GHOST STORIES FROM THE NORTH COUNTRY

being an account of some of the folklore and ghost stories of the northern counties of Northumberland and Durham and their adjacent lands

by

Henry Stuart Tegner M.A.

Edited by A.Price

AUTHOR'S NOTE

I have endeavoured withing the covers of this book to acknowledge the sources from which many of the incidents described have been derived. If I have failed to do so entirely adequately it is not from intent. There is so much available material and much of this is repetitive. To try and list every source of information would be in itself a considerable undertaking. I therefore take this opportunity to thank all those who have given me verbal records as well as those who have put me on to the trail of many published documents.

EDITOR'S NOTE

While much of the text is exactly as Henry Tegner wrote in 1974 in his pamphlet "Ghosts of the North Country", certain spelling corrections have been made, and some substitutions for French words (such as "Lambton pere" when discussing John Lambton's father) have been made. Hopefully this will not detract from Mr.Tegner's writing. From a personal point of view, the author's tenacity in tracking down leads from historic documents - in an era before the internet made such searching routine and relatively easy - is commendable and fascinating, although the references to fox hunting might be unpalatable to a more modern audience.

CONTENTS

Introduction	5
Some Lesser Ghosts of Northumberland, Durham and the adjacent counties	11
Land of Legend and Ballad	16
The Shadow on the Moor	22
The Old Moor House	25
The Lone Airman of Cheviot and the Spectre of the Boar	32
The Various Silkies	39
Meg o' Meldon	43
The White Lady of Cresswell	48
The Lambton Worm	53
The Pollard Worm	60
The White Lady of Dunstanburgh	63
The Ghostly Bridal of Featherstonehaugh	67
The Grey Man of Bellister	70
The White Lady of Blenkinsopp	72
The Spectre of Haughton Castle	75
Poltergeists at Callaly Castle and The Witch of Edlingham	77
The Vampire of Berwick and The Burning Man of Ebchester	81
The Hedley Kow and the Lark Hall Sprite	83
The Brown Man of the Moors and the Simonside Dwarfs	86
The Knaresdale Hall Ghost and the Headless Ghost of Watton Abbey	89
The Cauld Lad of Hylton	92
The Willington Ghost	95
The Lumley Ghost Story	98
The Long Pack	102
L'Envoi	108

INTRODUCTION

Looking back over the years I believe I have always been interested in the occult. By the word occult I do not necessarily mean ghosts as such. I think perhaps the better definition of occultism is simply the exploration and study of that which is hidden. Occultism to my mind does not necessarily imply a belief in the supernatural. It means rather the examination of much well authenticated phenomena which so far has not been adequately explained by the scientist.

My earliest recollection of the mysterious was an occurrence in Japan where I was born. I must have been seven or eight years old when I was staying with my uncle and aunt at a delightful bungalow on the beach at a little seaside village named Dzushi near the now thriving seaside resort of Kamakura. My uncle was Sophus Warming, then Danish consul in Japan. One day a Japanese fisherman was drowned in the bay of Dzushi. His body could not be found. That night a fleet of little sampans set out to sea whilst each vessel had protruding over the bow a basket-work cage containing a cockerel. When a boat passed over the corpse the bird would crow, I was told. At dawn next day the fleet came home. The body had been recovered. A cockerel had crowed.

When one has spent much time studying nature and wild-life as I have done I believe that one is instinctively attracted by the unusual. The unknown and the mysterious, it would seem to me, are more likely to reveal themselves in the unpopulated places rather than in the hurly-burly of densely packed towns and the streets of our cities. One can hardly imagine seeing a ghost during the mid-day rush hour in Market Street or Blackett Street in a city like Newcastle upon Tyne. Spirits, if there are any such, would seem to me to prefer to exercise themselves on this earth of ours in the quiet hours of dawn and then again towards dusk in what one could fairly describe as empty places. Tranquility and a serene atmosphere would somehow appear to be a more appropriate background for a proper examination of such phenomena of the occult as telepathy, astral projections, apports and the many other aspects of the Great Unknown. Much of my spare time has been spent in the dawn and dusk studying wild-life, but rather to my disappointment I have never encountered anything abnormally weird during these happy expeditions. Other places which would seem to me to be conducive to supernatural happenings are the high hills. That mountains can influence one's thoughts and ego I have no doubt whatsoever. The rarity of the air at altitude may have something to do with the development of paranormal perception. The Tibetans have always been a mystic people and the Himalayas have usually been accepted as a sort of focal land for those with spiritualistic leanings.

Spiritualism today has an enormous following. In the past, and also at the present time, many eminent men have professed a belief in the existence of disembodied spirits - ghosts to give them their more commonplace names. One only has to mention that men of the calibre of the great scientist Sir Oliver Lodge, the eminent chemist Sir William Crookes, discoverer of thallium and ammonium, F.W.H. Myers, Professor William James of Harvard University, a philosopher and psychologist of outstanding reputation, and the Reverend Vale Owen, author of The Life Beyond the Vale, were all "believers in ghosts". Later, and perhaps more flamboyantly, there was Sir Arthur Conan Doyle, creator of Sherlock Holmes and an outstanding spiritualist. Lord Dowding, who is now rightly credited with having won the Battle of Britain in the 1939-45 war, was a dedicated spiritualist. His book on communication with the dead entitled Many Mansions has gone into no less than ten editions. Both Dowding and, before him, Conan Doyle, believed in fairies and neither was a madman.

It might be as well here to define a spiritualist. A spiritualist, as I understand it, is a person who believes in the existence of discarnate spirits and in their ability to manifest themselves to living beings by way of apparition, physical phenomena or intelligible communication. Swedenborg, a Swede as his name implies, is now credited with being the founder of the Spiritualistic Creed. He it was who wrote, what one might call the spiritualist's New Testament, the Heavenly Arcana. Like so many other confirmed spiritualists Swedenborg did not accept the life-hereafter until he was well into middle age. He was, in fact, fifty-five when he became a true believer. Born in 1688, Swedenborg died in 1772, aged eighty-four. There is a vast literature on the occult beginning with the Bible which is certainly one of the most profoundly occult works in existence. Spiritualism, on occasion, has been disclaimed as an accepted religion but for what reasons it is hard to say, for after all a religion is merely a system of faith and worship. Spiritualism, like so many other faiths, has various tenets which need not be considered in this brief introduction. The multitude of books which have been published on such subjects as spiritualism, occultism, clairvoyance, mesmerism, telepathy, astrology, re-incarnation and ghosts is well demonstrated by a brief survey of the card index system in any public library. Under such headings the enquirer at Newcastle's City Library will find enough to keep him reading for the rest of his life. Although the literature of the supernatural is enormous much of it is practically useless for evidential purposes. Facts, indeed, are cited but the records of them are all too often fallible and imperfect. Strangely enough, there is not a great plethora of books which deal specifically with the ghosts and allied occult subjects of this north country of ours. Exceptions are *William Henderson's Folk Lore of the Northern Counties* (1879), *Richardson's Local Historian's Table Book* and the quite admirable five volumes of *The Monthly Chronicle* dating from 1887 to 1891.

Ghosts are a part of nearly all the better known religions such as Presbyterianism, Roman Catholicism, Buddhism et alii. Presbyterians maintain that the souls of believers are at their death made perfect in holiness, and their bodies being still united to Christ do rest in their graves until the resurrection. We have the evidence of the various apostles Matthew, Mark, Luke and John of the violent death by crucifixion of Christ and then his subsequent burial, or entombment, and his resurrection after three days when his disincarnated spirit was observed by Mary and the disciples. This surely then must have been the spirit or ghost of Jesus - the Holy Ghost. The actual account of the death of Jesus, his entombment, the subsequent removal of his body and the eventual resurrection of his soul varies slightly according to the gospels of these four men but in essence the story is the same. Therefore if you should profess to be a Christian, who believes in God and the Bible, you must also credit the existence of ghosts in spite of the fact that in 999 cases out of 1,000, if not an even much greater ratio, you may never have seen, heard or felt a spirit from Beyond.

The Roman Catholic Church, from the earliest times, has maintained a belief in the resurrection of the material body. Most Roman Catholics today still fervently credit miracles; one only has to look at the millions of this faith who crowd annually to such places as Lourdes in search of a miraculous cure - and it must be faced that some marvellous recoveries, from diseases medically regarded as quite incurable, have come about as a result of sufferers' visits to such places. Towards the end of the last century there would seem to have been a considerable resurgence of interest in the supernatural, this has certainly continued. It was in 1882 that The Society for Psychical Research was founded. Its first President was Henry Sedgwick, Professor of Moral Philosophy in the University of Cambridge. Other prominent persons subsequently became Presidents including Professor Balfour Stewart, A.J. Balfour, Professor William James of Harvard, Sir William Crookes, Sir Oliver Lodge and Bishop Boyd Carpenter. One of the main functions of this eminent Society is to probe the unknown. It issues Proceedings which are available to the public. Nearly all the material contained in these papers is of very considerable interest to one with an inquisitive mind.

Long before the Society came into existence man, of course, had tried to pierce the vale beyond life. History shows that not only the Christian and his Bible but others as well, such as the Greek and Roman intelligentsia were believers in a life beyond - Plutarch, Pliny, Socrates and Cicero took the presence of ghosts for granted. In the course of recent years I have made a particular study of Pliny, for he was a most observant and excellent naturalist. One suspects that this Roman historian would have been truly amazed if anyone were to doubt the existence of spectres, phantoms and other such ghostly forms.

Spiritualists today still actively pursue any physical manifestations of after-life such as the nebulous ectoplasm of which, some scientists believe, ghosts consist; cases of unexpected noises and rappings, the mysterious movement of solid objects and other occult demonstrations all come within the spiritualist's inquisitive scope. Today the subject of astrology is remarkably popular and its association with prediction and clairvoyance. Opinion polls show that young people tend to believe increasingly in fortune-telling and the forecasts of the palm reader. The soothsayer has never had it so good. Publishers continue to bring out books on black-magic and the paranormal. Some of the bookshelves containing the various paper-back series have sections which are devoted to the ghostly. In America today there are believed to be no less than 5,000 professional astrologers with a consulting clientèle of nearly ten million people a year. Nearly a thousand newspapers, with a daily circulation of forty millions, have a horoscope column. Superstitions still linger. How many of us can brush aside, without a qualm of any sort, the age-old credos which warn us that should a single magpie be seen our luck is out or that spilt salt, unless a peck be cast over the left shoulder, bodes ill. Then there is one's normal aversion to walk under a ladder, or to view a new moon through glass. A gift knife cuts friendship unless paid for with a penny-piece. Thirteen is still considered an unlucky number. A horse shoe nailed the wrong way up means your luck will run down the heel pieces instead of being withheld within its crescent hoop when correctly hung. There is a fundamental urge in most people to be thrilled and surprised by any phenomena which does not abide by the rules we are acquainted with. Personally, I still find magic in the working of the radio and more lately television. Here in their individual spheres man has been able to break all the rules and to force men's voices through masses of steel and concrete to an individual's auditory senses. Live pictures are now brought to one's fireside through space and through matter. What could be more wonderful? Certainly such phenomena would have been far more unbelievable to our forefathers than such things as survival after death. I suppose an electrician could explain the mundane nature of the radio and the telly, but I doubt whether I could grasp the full ways of their working. The age of miracles is surely far from past when one considers medicine's strides in the transplantation of such vital human organs as the heart and kidneys. Men have journeyed to the moon to walk upon that planet's surface. Incidentally, the black and white television pictures of the astronauts' meanderings on the lunar sphere are as near man's past conception of ghost-forms as makes no matter. I have never deliberately tried to probe into the Unknown - the Unknown, for lack of a better word, has very rarely, I believe, come to me. Sometimes, admittedly, to be later explained. That there is much in telepathy I am certain. How often does one write a letter to a particular friend to find one's letters have crossed, and on receipt both missives have expressed similar thoughts. I suppose a psychologist or some learned analyst of the human brain could tell you how thoughts can be transmitted over immense distances. Many have attempted to do so, But to me this sort of happening is still marvellous and it savours of the supernatural.

At a time when so many people are becoming less sceptical about ghosts it is perhaps ironical that there should seem to be less of them about - certainly fewer, at least, of the headless horsemen and grey lady varieties but sightings nevertheless continue to be reported. The experience of seeing a ghost is now cynically ascribed to some individual hallucinations and most serious investigators suggest that the vision is extra-sensory. If there is such a thing as a sixth sense, and many of us believe that there is, then surely there is a strong case for further exploration for it is no use behaving as if such does not, or could not, exist. When it was suggested to me that I should write a book about ghosts I was at first quite flabbergasted, but then I began to turn the project over in my mind. The subject started to intrigue; and then it became absorbing. It has caused me to venture on the vast fringe of the literature of the occult, it has taken me to haunted places and all-in-all it has provided me with a new field of adventure not entirely dissociated, in many ways, with a lifelong study of nature in its many varied and attractive spheres.

SOME LESSER GHOSTS OE NORTHUMBERLAND, DURHAM AND THE ADJACENT COUNTIES

This is a book which attempts to deal with some ghost stories and legends of the northern counties of Northumberland and Durham and the adjacent lands thereto. The surprising thing to me is that there are not more ghosts about up here in the far north of England, and for that matter in the Scottish Border Counties. We have here surely natural spirit terrain. There are still in existence hundreds of ancient peles, fortalices, ruined castles and we have the Roman Wall and all its marvellous historical associations. Why are there not more Roman ghosts? For certainly the occupying forces of the Roman Empire had their soothsayers, clairvoyants and most were spiritualists in the sense that they would have surely believed in the existence of ghosts. The history of the Wall is certainly a drum and trumpet affair from the time when the *buccina* of the Batavian cohort first rang out over the backbone of Northern England - ghosts and legends one would imagine there would be in plenty, but strangely such are lacking. The story of Northumbria's hauntings comes much later and it begins with the advent of Christianity and St. Aidan.

Rudyard Kipling's *Puck of Pook's Hill* has its location as the Wall. Kipling could write a mystical story as well as anyone. One suspects that Rudyard Kipling, in company with Conan Doyle, was sympathetic to the occult. He must have had an enormous experience of the mystic during his many years spent in India, where such things as thought transference, disincarnation and other trance phenomena are common. I suspect that castles like Bothal, Halton, Ogle, Harbottle and surely Alnwick all have their ghosts but I have not been particularly successful in finding out much about them. On the other hand there are some old and well established, alleged haunted places such as Haughton, Bellister, Edlingham, Dunstanburgh, Blenkinsopp and a number of others. Why is there no ghost in Lindisfarne Castle? A really romantic, sea-girt bastion if ever there is one; but perhaps Lindisfarne has not got a sufficiently horrific history, for what legends there are about this romantic-looking erection appear to be, if anything, rather jolly ones with no records of murder or mayhem. Holy Island, however, has its ghost, that of St. Cuthbert who is said at low tides on moonlit nights to sit on a boulder below the little peninsula of Hobthrush, opposite the old lifeboat shed, fashioning the now famous Cuddy's beads into necklaces for his rosary. St. Cuthbert's beads are little round button-like fossils, the stems of beautiful little sea-crinoids, or feather stars, a primitive form of marine creature. Beachcombers below Hobthrush may still find these little fossils on the beaches there. One of the earliest legends connected with the occult was surely the vision St. Cuthbert was said to have seen when he was a shepherd's lad in the Cheviots, or the Lammermuirs. No one seems to be quite sure of the actual site of this visitation which caused Cuthbert to become a monk.

Cadwaller J. Bates in his *History of Northumberland* gives a good account of St. Cuthbert's call. This somewhat eccentric author, and ardent Roman Catholic, was the great uncle of the present Thomas Bates of Nilston Rigg. Cadwaller J. Bates had all the iron gates around Langley Castle, the Bates' ancestral estate, painted purple and he is said to have drunk a toast daily "To the King Over the Water", being an ardent supporter of the Pretender. Bates describes how Cuthbert, out tending his sheep in the hills, sees a vision in the sky of angels bearing the soul of St. Aidan. He prostrates himself in the form of a cross and prays fervently. At the time of this vision St. Aidan was said to be in his death throes at the castle of Bamburgh. Cuthbert, having duly had the call, quickly travelled on foot to the nearest monastery at Melrose where he was welcomed by St. Boisil and made an acolyte, which appears to have been a form of cheap labour for the monks, although my dictionary says that an acolyte is a priest's attendant. This vision of St. Cuthbert's is interesting in a number of ways. Firstly because the legend bears a striking resemblance to the Shepherds' vision of Christ's lowly birth in a manger, and their summons there, and also it would seem that by what we now call telepathy the actual dying of St. Aidan, first saint of Lindisfarne, was transmitted to the chosen Cuthbert who was eventually himself to become a Saint of Lindisfarne.

Langley Castle has its own ghost, said to be a coach and horses driven by a headless man. I have not seen this apparition myself, nor have I met anyone else who has done so. There are quite a number of what might be termed lesser ghosts, or hauntings, within the counties of Northumberland and Durham and some of these have been described by William Henderson in his delightful *Folklore of the Northern Counties* published in 1879. The farm of Dalton Hill Head, once owned by the Hedley family of Newcastle and which was subsequently sold to a Mr. Collingwood of Dissington, was said to be haunted, although few exact details are given. William Henderson says that a Mary Henderson, a relative of the inventor George Stephenson, was then housekeeper at Dalton Hill Head. *She kept a big mastiff dog continuously with her who would cringe at the sounds of pattering feet and the voices of little children.* Later, Mary was to find the bones of infants amongst old clothes and hat boxes in the attic. The removal of these remains presumably was sufficient to exorcise the ghosts. Such exorcisms are by no means unusual. William Henderson incidentally was not only a good editor, for he has collected a fine assembly of records on folklore, but he was also evidently an ardent angler for he wrote an attractive treatise entitled *My Life as an Angler.*

Another source of information concerning the local occult is the admirable nineteenth century magazine *The Monthly Chronicle* and here in volume five, dated 1S91, are recorded no less than seven hauntings in one short article. The first account concerns the appearance of a murdered man near the site of the old railway station opposite the George Hotel at Chollerford. Then there is the story of the gluttonous farmer, by the name of Bell, who always had a round of beef by his bedside. Bell is described as a big fat man who in life was both voluble and profane. No exact location is given as to where Bell lived except that he is mentioned as a Border farmer. After his death, presumably from over indulgence, his ghost was frequently seen by one Kirsty Weatherstone, a servant in the house. In death Bell became silent. No one appears to have been particularly fearful of Bell's spectre; driving about the countryside in his gig the folk would say "There goes the old thief again!" Bell's seems to have been a jolly ghost.

A more macabre ghost is that of another Border farmer, named Dunlop, who was said to have starved his first wife to death and then taken to his bed his much younger serving maid whom he subsequently wed. The younger woman also predeceased her husband. After this, wife number one came to haunt Dunlop sitting opposite him by the fireside. Katy Winchester, a local woman, stated she had often seen the ghost of Dunlop's first wife. There is no record of when this twice- wedded agriculturist himself left this mortal coil.

A pedlar was the victim of a murderous innkeeper in a small Border town, the name of which is not mentioned. The pedlar was believed to have been carrying a good deal of money on him. He was seen to go into the inn but never to re-appear. The innkeeper, a poor man until then, subsequently became wealthy and his son wealthier still. Eventually the younger man bought a big house; but always on the anniversary of his father's suspected murder of the pedlar bells would sound throughout the house.

There is also the tragic tale of the hind's wife who was overburdened with too many children and in distraction murdered the last to arrive during the time of the harvest full moon. This poor creature became demented. Her ghost was then seen to appear regularly when harvest time came round. The period of the full-moon is linked closely in much of the occult as a period of high-hauntings. That there is some lunar power prevalent at its periodical zenith would appear to be possible. Pedlars continually feature as victims of murder and they sometimes also assume the role of murderers themselves. Pedlars in the past were carriers of goods and, at times, considerable amounts of money. They were the commercial travellers of a previous age, carrying not only goods and samples but gossip, news and ghostly tales as well. Probably the best-known and most exciting story of the death of a pedlar is

The Long Pack, about which more later in this book. *The Monthly Chronicle* in its article on hauntings also tells of a Rothbury farmer whose wife killed another pedlar, who was carrying much loose cash, with a heavy churn-staff. In collaboration with her husband the body of the traveller was buried in a well. The farmer soon died from a fall from his horse. The ghost of the pedlar came to haunt the wife who eventually confessed to a priest. This would appear to have been a case of a guilty conscience rather than a spiritual visitation resulting in remorse. Wilson, also a farmer, from Stockton, became very drunk one day when at the market. On his way home he was drowned in the River Tees. His body was eventually recovered, but not his hat. A hatless figure was then regularly seen near the ford across the river. A local Methodist preacher named John Orton has claimed to have seen this apparition.

It is perhaps not altogether surprising that so little detail has been given in these accounts of nineteenth century ghosts and hauntings concerning names, places and the ghostly phenomena themselves, for people then, as many today, did not wish particularly to be associated with the ghostly. This, either for fear of being laughed at, or some other perfectly sensible reason such as that the properties, allegedly visited by the supernatural, are inclined to fall in value or are not easily let or sold. The uncanny still has a fearful power in spite of modern cynicism and the wider spread of knowledge.

If anyone thinks that ghosts and hauntings went out in our northern counties with the last century they should surely think again. In the month of January, 1971 *The Journal*, a Newcastle daily paper of the Thomson Group, gave accounts of two haunted houses; one a hotel in Beadnell and another of a council house in Lanchester, County Durham. The latter is particularly interesting. In this case details of the number of the house, its name, if it had one, etcetera, are tactfully not given, but the description of the nature of the hauntings and the various efforts made to exorcise the spirit are all there in detail. I quote verbatim.

"Frightened 'ghost' family may ask for new home", say the headlines,
and then,
"A family of eight will ask a County Durham Rural Council to rehouse them if a third attempt fails to rid their home of a ghost. It first appeared on Christmas Eve and has forced the family to flee from their four-bedroom house in Lanchester. Two vicars, the Reverend James Lovell, of Esh, and Canon George Beckwith of Lanchester, have visited the home and tried to exorcise the spirit. They both believe in its presence".

    This first attempt at exorcism apparently met with little success for the B.B.C. on its eight o'clock news bulletin on 21st January, 1971, described the visit to this council house in Lanchester of one of their film units. The members of this team stayed in the house from midnight to 5 a.m. The leader of the unit and his team came away not having actually seen a ghost, but they appear to have both sensed and felt one, the atmosphere at certain times becoming icy cold so that their various items of equipment became difficult to handle. The leader, a Mr.Green, was certainly very convincing over the air whilst he was being interviewed. Ghosts and hauntings would seem to be ever with us; they are evidently not phenomena of the past, and like old soldiers they never seem to die, only to gradually fade away. The exorcism of ghosts, hauntings and other supernatural phenomena has been practised in the past, as well as today, by the exponents and priests of nearly all religions. And in many cases it would appear that exorcism, or the
casting out of evil spirits by invocation, works.

LAND OF LEGEND AND BALLAD

    In a previous book of mine *Charm of the Cheviots* (1970) I briefly dealt with a number of legends and ghost stories which are closely associated with this part of the country. Here again there are old records as well as recent ones. One story in particular which appealed to me was that of a party of young people who went up the lower reaches of the Cheviot Hills on a camping expedition. *The Sunday Sun* of 1st August, 1965, gives a good account of their adventures. The party consisted of two girls and four boys who pitched two tents, one for the ladies presumably and one for the gentlemen, beside a burn in the Alwine valley. On Sunday night, 16th July, or more accurately Monday morning at 1.15, both tents began to vibrate and the earth shudder, although there was no trace of wind. Both parties emerged from their bivouacs to investigate the cause of their disturbance when a great ghostly figure, stated to have been over eight feet in height, was seen to disappear up-river. This sounds like some hoax plus possibly a slight seismic shock, but the curious thing is that there is an old legend which tells of a sheep-stealer who was hanged many years ago near the very place where the teenagers had their camp! The ghost of the sheep-stealer is said to walk on the midnight of 18th July, very close in time to the July date when these young people claim to have seen their apparition. Tents, of course, because of their structure and the material of which they are nowadays made, can boom, hum, shudder and sometimes also screech! There is another old legend which says that when the dour north-easterly winds come up the Cheviot valleys the screams are to be heard of the lonely pedlar who had lost his way in the hills and then tumbled over a precipice, and who died hung by the straps of his pack which got caught on a projecting rock. This is surely a separate spirit to that of the sheep-stealer, although the haunted localities are not far apart.

The Henhole, or Hell-Hole, to the east of the summit of Cheviot is the favoured site of many an old tale. It can be quite an eerie place. Abel Chapman, famed naturalist, author and sportsman of the North Tyne valley, has called it "that eerie abyss yclept the Henhole". One old yarn describes how a party of hunters engaged in the pursuit of a roebuck were lured into this abyss by the sweetest music ever heard, but once in the ravine they became imprisoned and could never find their way out. This legend is remarkably similar to the more popular version of Harry Hotspur's hunting in the Cheviots when he and his pack of hounds got holed up in the

Hell Hole. A landslide is said to have overtaken the pack and their huntsman. The story goes on to say that Percy and his hounds now await the call of the hunter's horn to release them from their age-long incarceration.

Oddly enough, my old friend and ex-M.F.H. Jake Robson of the Border Hunt once ran a fox to ground in the Henhole. On taking out his horn to call hounds to him the fox, to everyone's astonishment, sprang down from the crevice, in which it had concealed itself, right into the jaws of the hounds below. Perhaps the fox had encountered the deceased spirits of the Percy party entombed in their "eerie abyss"?

William Weaver Tomlinson, in his *Comprehensive Guide to the County of Northumberland* (circa 1912) and reprinted in 1967, says that the final scene of the ballad in Fred Sheldon's *Minstrelsy of the English Border* under the title "Black Adam of Cheviot" is laid in the Henhole. The poem tells how the leading character - a notorious freebooter known as "The Rider of Cheviot" - burst in upon a wedding gathering at nearby Wooperton and whilst the bridegroom was engaged in fetching the priest, he did then strip the women present of their jewels, ravish the bride and finally murder her by stabbing. The bridegroom meanwhile returns just in time to hear Black Adam's laugh of scorn. The unfortunate man then tore off his bride's gory kerchief to vow revenge on the foul murderer. There now begins a dramatic chase until the hunted reiver arrives at the brink of a chasm in the hills when by a desperate leap of seven yards, or more, he succeeds in gaining his lair, a cave in the side of a steep cliff. Sheldon's poem goes on to tell how the bereaved bridegroom and Black Adam finally come to grips on the ledge of the Henhole to fall as one - locked in death. So far as I know there are no recorded ghosts of Black Adam, the bridegroom, or the ravished bride. It is a pity, as all these characters would appear to have in life just the stuff from which eventually good ghosts emanate.

I was reading a book recently which I had taken from the Newcastle City Library bookshelves. This was entitled *Ghosts* and had been published in 1965 under the authorship of Dennis

Bardens. Bardens briefly relates the story of the ghost of the appalling Lord Soulis, a notorious priest of witchcraft and devil worship. Soulis' story is well-known and most of his foul deeds were supposed to have taken place at Hermitage Castle in Roxburghshire within sight, as it were, of the Cheviot massif. I quote.

"A particularly malevolent ghost, of whose appearance innumerable accounts exist at various periods, is that of 'Terrible William', otherwise Lord Soulis, who practised black magic at his castle. In pursuance of his evil rites, so local tradition goes, he would kidnap local children, incarcerate them in his dungeons, murder them and use their blood in appalling rituals. When at last news of his misdeeds became common knowledge in the village, the people took him prisoner, bound him in chains and threw him into a cauldron of boiling lead, After this his shade was frequently to be seen about the environs of the castle, re-enacting his filthy practices".

The story of Lord Soulis' ghost has been often repeated; it has become, one might say, one of the classic Border ghost yarns. Hence its inclusion here.

Herbert L. Honeyman in his book *Northumberland* says, page 195, that "Ghosts are rather a feature of this corner of the county (South Tyne) with an entire hunting party at Pinkie's Cleugh; a treasure guarding dwarf at Thirlwell Castle; a black dog at Blenkinsopp Hall, a white lady at Blenkinsopp Castle, and a grey man at Bellister Castle". Our ghosts are, however, not by any means confined to the South Tyne area although this is splendid ghost country. They wander from Tweed to Tees and beyond.

Northumberland, Durham and the Border counties of Scotland have all had, in the past century, powerful and most excellent recorders of romance, poetry and the mystic. Three men in particular, all closely contemporary, as the table below shows, aided and built up a substantial literature which has to do with our folklore and the romantic tales of the countryside. These men were brilliant, attractive writers. The most famous was Sir Walter Scott. As a poet James Hogg, generally known as The Ettrick Shepherd, is now accepted as one of Scotland's most revered poets. Robert Surtees of Mainsforth, County Durham who wrote *The History of the County of Durham* is perhaps less well-known in the international sphere but he was nonetheless a brilliant scholar who appears to have been able to more than keep up his end with people like Walter Scott. The dates of birth and death of all these three writers coincide very closely.

James Hogg : 1770 - 1835
Walter Scott : 1771 - 1832
Robert Surtees : 1779 - 1834

All three men were acquainted and corresponded frequently.

Robert Surtees of Mainsforth should not be confused with his more popular cousin Robert Smith Surtees of Hamsterley, County Durham, who wrote *Jorrock's Jaunts and Jollities* and many other now famous hunting novels. Robert Smith was younger than his cousin of Mainsforth, having been born at the Riding, Northumberland in 1805. Both men had a strong streak of the practical joker and, let it be said, cynic as well, in their make-up. Surtees, elder and younger, not infrequently used their sharp pens to take the micky out of various people. One wonders, at times, why they seem to have taken such a delight in knocking others. Robert Smith Surtees' characters are often brazen caricatures of well-known personalities. His Pomponius Ego, Facey Romford, Jogglebury Crowdy, Soapy Sponge, Sloedolager and Lucy Glitters were all based on real life characters and in their descriptions, funny as nearly all of them are, there is a considerable amount of "vitriol." Surtees, the elder's, most elaborate piece of quixotic puckishness was when he went to immense trouble to supply Walter Scott with a series of bogus ballads for Scott's much beloved *Minstrelsy of the Scottish Border*. The various legends, poems and ballads concocted by Surtees at Mainsforth were undoubtedly works of art in themselves and they were duly annotated with references of origin, authorship and location. Scott, then practically unknown, was earnestly in search of original material. Surtees, an antiquarian and also historian, educated at Christ Church, Oxford, afterwards called to the Middle Temple, was able to supply the goods. Ancient tales and poems like *The Death of Featherstonehaugh, Bartram's Dirge* and *Lord Derwentwater's Goodnight* were superb forgeries. George Taylor in his *A Memoir of Robert Surtees, Esq., M.A., F.S.A.*, gives an interesting account of Surtees' spurious ballads and how he successfully foisted these on to Scott who in all good faith used some of the material in *Marmion*. It is certainly a little surprising to learn that when Scott finally became aware that he had been duped he was charming about it, not being a bit bitter. He merely suggested that the material was of such intrinsic merit that it was worthy of inclusion in any romantic work! All this is inclined to make one somewhat suspicious of the many legends and ghost stories which have come down to us via writings of men such as these.

James Hogg was a delightful poet and raconteur, in so far as the two northern English counties are concerned. His epic tale *The Long Pack* located in Northumberland is surely a delightful anecdote.

Sir Walter Scott, one senses, was an ardent romantic; he also loved a gruesome ghoul and a good ghost. Many of his tales include references to the occult and the mystic.

One other author who has used, on occasion, the Cheviot range, or the nearby Lammermuir Hills, for his scenes of action was John Buchan, first Baron Tweedsmuir. Buchan in his *Moon Endureth*, one of his earliest books, describes a mystic spot he calls *The Green Glen*. This surely is located somewhere amongst the grey rounded hills of the Border regions whilst *The Riding of Ninemile Burn* might well have taken place in Northumberland. Most of the stories, so excellently and mystically told by Buchan, and which are included in *The Moon Endureth*, originally appeared in *Blackwood's Magazine*, a great source then, as it is now, of many authentic, or fictional, accounts of the occult. Incidentally in this book of Buchan's, Lord Soulis of Hermitage Castle and his evil doings are given a mention.

John Buchan was not only a prolific and delightful writer but he was also a man of many parts who eventually became Governor General of Canada. When I was on an international course for officers at Balliol, Oxford, during the 1939-45 war, we were invited by Lady Tweedsmuir to visit her at nearby Boar's Hill. It was an exciting hour for me when I was shown John Buchan's own study with his various books, which he wrote in longhand, all bound and arrayed around the shelves.

THE SHADOW ON THE MOOR

The Shadow on the Moor first appeared in *Blackwood's Magazine* in 1931, a source, as stated in the previous chapter, of much exciting material concerning the occult and the supernatural. This long, short story was then eventually published in book form. Written by Alan Ian, Eighth Duke of Northumberland, father of the present Duke, it can now be classed as a modern legend of this northern county. I have placed it early in this book because I feel that it is one of the best, if not the best, "ghost" stories ever written about this part of the country. The descriptions of the countryside, the weather conditions and the whole atmosphere of a thrilling fox-hunt can scarcely be beaten. The story of *The Shadow on the Moor* is surely pure fiction but in its telling it comes close to fact.

The Henhole, as such, is not specifically mentioned but one cannot help but assume from the detailed description of the hunt itself, its direction, and the persons described, that the hunted fox, or foxes, finally lured their maniac huntsman to his death in that "eerie abyss yclept the Henhole". Imaginary names have been used throughout but to one who knows the country-side and the various packs of hounds which are established here, it is not difficult to follow the hunt from find to finish and to locate the points and the various places through which the phantom fox, or foxes, led the pack and their pursuing huntsman to their doom. The hunt itself is obviously a typical north country pack; it could be the Jed Forest, the College Valley, the North Northumberland, the West Percy or the Percy. Because the original hunted fox found was at Cuthbertsborough, which from its description must surely have been Dunstanburgh, I take the fictional hunt involved to have been the Percy.

A story re-told is never as good as the original but as *The Shadow* is not, by any means, an easy book to obtain today, I shall venture to condense this quite superb tale. The story is told at second-hand, the author relating that he had it from one Armstrong, a farmer, whose father had ridden in the actual hunt and who had witnessed its final disastrous end.

The landed Squire, who had been Master of this unnamed pack of hounds, had grown old and as his physical capacity dwindled he was forced to engage a professional huntsman to carry the horn. The man eventually selected was one Tom Fletcher, known as Black Tom because of his swarthy complexion. Tom Fletcher was said to have been born of a gipsy woman by the roadside who had then died in childbirth. Who his father was no one knew. He, like his mother, was probably a gipsy, or Faa as these folk were once known in the far north of England. Previous to his engagement with the Squire's hounds Black Tom had been whipper-in to a hill pack in Roxburghshire. He was universally credited with being a man who was a wonder with both hounds and horses. He was also evidently a man of violent temper but a powerful rider with an instinctive knowledge of animal psychology. One evening, after a long day's hunting, Tom Fletcher was coming home in the gloaming with his hounds and his whipper-in, Jim Murray, in attendance. A hound was found to be missing. Murray was immediately sent back by Black Tom to find the missing bitch. Before reaching the kennels Murray turned up without having found the lost hound. Black Tom, now in a complete fury struck out at his whipper-in with the hammer-head of his massive hunting crop. Murray was killed but there was no direct evidence of murder as the horse Murray had been mounted on was found riderless some time later. Black Tom insisted that he had never seen his whip again *after he had been sent off to seek the lost hound.* Murray's young wife, however, was obsessed with a strong suspicion; so sure was she that her husband had been done to death that she proceeded to accuse Black Tom, but to no purpose.

One day, a short time afterwards, hounds were out hunting in the low country towards the North Sea. After a wet and fruitless morning with not a fox to be found, it was decided, as a last draw, to try the extensive gorse covers to the east of the old ruined castle of Cuthbertsborough. This I feel certain is Dunstanburgh for the description of the terrain and its location almost exactly fits this site. By now there were few riders left with hounds, most of the field having gone home. One of those still out was Armstrong's father who was the only man to leave a verbal record of what now took place. A fox was eventually roused in the gorse covers to break out to the landward, or east side of the old castle. At this moment a piercing holler was heard which to all present sounded exactly like the voice of the recently dead Jim Murray. At the same time the silhouette of a figure was seen with his cap in the air - the ghost of the deceased whipper-in? This phantom was never seen again during the course of the ensuing hunt although his voice was to be heard on more than one occasion. Hounds broke cover in full cry. The fox made inland towards what is now the A.1 road to Berwick on Tweed. There now follows a vivid account of this amazing fox hunt. The pace was fast and the country, as it was traversed, became more and more wild. Gradually the small field of followers began to fall out. Whenever hounds checked on the line a piercing holler from a quite invisible being would put them right. Armstrong, in telling his story, believed that the pack hunted more than one fox but the line never altered, always leading towards the hills. The great pace and the length of the hunt were telling on the horses, but Black Tom rode as if the Devil was after him. Which undoubtedly he was, so far as the huntsman was concerned, for Black Tom would keep looking over his shoulder, crouching down at the same time close to his sweating horse's neck, as if he was being pursued by some invisible body. Armstrong had said that his father saw what appeared to be a small black cloud in an otherwise clear blue sky hang over Black Tom as he drove his now jaded horse harder and harder. The end comes when hounds reach the lip of a ravine called The Glitters; this I believe is the author's fictional name for the Henhole. The Pack pour, as a single entity, into the chasm and close on their heels in a state of mad terror Black Tom follows to crash to his death hundreds of feet below. The description of this hunt, the weird *hollers* of the deceased whipper-in and the eerie appearance of the pursuing shadow are all spine-chillingly described. The final *whoo-o-whoop* of the haunted huntsman as he goes to his death in the Glitters is bloodcurdling although it is only an onomatopoeic word set down in cold print. I have measured the distance of this hunt on an ordnance survey map with a scale of half an inch to the mile. I make this to be a twenty mile point. A very good run and as written up not much farther as hounds actually ran for they went very straight. A good hunt certainly but not an impossible one surely. In one of *Horse and Hound's* hunting reports in 1971 there is a description of a hunt of over twenty miles, as hounds ran, of the Percy Hunt when Claxton, their professional huntsman, was hunting the bitch pack. Found by Burnie House this stout fox ended up at Fiddler's Elbow in the Morpeth country. This is but one factual account of a number of somewhat similar lengthy runs which take place every season, so that the story in The Shadow of this disastrous fox hunt is by no means fantastic or abnormal. Whether the real Glitters was the eventual scene of the catastrophy or the Henhole is really immaterial, in so far as the distance is concerned, for the Glitters shown on a map of the Cheviot district is only a very short distance, as the raven is alleged to fly, from the Henhole itself.

The Shadow on the Moor is a fine tale well told.

THE OLD MOOR HOUSE

The Old Moor House is no more. It is just a pile of tumbled stones. Some of them square and massive. Amongst this rubble tall oak and elm trees grow. Before it was destroyed the Old Moor House stood at the head of the little stream known as the

Wellhope Burn. The Wellhope has its source in a spring within sight of the rounded heathery knoll called Shirlah Pike. The people of the Old Moor House would have undoubtedly obtained their drinking water from this spring in the hills. Just before you get to this ruin from the south there is an old, slightly hump-backed stone bridge across the Wellhope, sufficiently broad to allow a coach and horses to pass over it. Below the bridge the burn drops steeply then cascades over a fall into a deep gully, or ravine. A viaduct carries the present main A.697 road over this chasm.

The ancient Roman road from Newcastle to Wooler passes by the grounds of the Old Moor House. It was, in fact, the main road from Newcastle to Coldstream, over the Border in Scotland, until comparatively recently when it was slightly bye-passed by A.697. The Roman Legions used this road and so undoubtedly, much later, did the warring factions of England and Scotland. Later still, in times of so-called peace, cattle drovers, rich merchants in their coaches and other travellers came along this route. It appears to have been a good hunting place for highwaymen and robbers. Now numbered A.697 the road closely follows the Devil's Causeway which was the name man gave to this highway, many years ago.

How, when and why this old mansion came to be destroyed I have never been able to ascertain. There is, in fact, very little historical evidence about the place at all. Although I have quite an extensive library, containing a fair number of books about this part of the country, I can find practically nothing about the Old Moor House or its story. One small volume entitled *Border Bye-Paths* by someone who has written under the pen-name of "Geordie Bell" has mentioned that, at one time, between Greystone Knowe and Wellhope Knowe there was an old inn at the roadside which had an evil reputation. This building, the author says, but does not state when, was destroyed and a new inn built at the cross-roads farther north. The so-called New Inn still exists. "Geordie Bell" mentions that opposite this house of ill repute (The Old Moor House) one of the many Border gallows used to stand.

The Devil's Causeway at the Old Moor House.

This gruesome reminder of human destruction has also disappeared although there are other such relics, still extant, within the county, and one in particular at Harwood which is a somewhat similar situation to the moor of Rimside, the site of the Old Moor House.

W. W. Tomlinson in his *Comprehensive Guide to Northumberland* mentions of Rimside that "This dreary waste was formerly much infested by highwaymen, who committed numerous outrages on travellers passing between Alnwick or Wooler and Morpeth".

I came upon another item of interest about this place from an old copy of the now-defunct Newcastle Magazine. The article was mainly about moor birds and it dealt at some length with both the red grouse and the black grouse, curlews, golden plover and snipe. The writer of the article had added a tailpiece to his short literary composition which was dated 1824, and which read:

> *"O'er Rimside, should the journey lie*
> *he'd flat refuse to go"*

    This couplet I have no doubt whatever referred to the site known as the Old Moor House. Why anyone should have ever built a house up on this bleak place is difficult to understand. The site is exposed to all the winds. There is practically no shelter. In the winter snow lies for long periods and because of its altitude, some 850 feet above sea-level, it gets the full force of any north or north-easterly storms which sometimes sweep over this countryside. I sometimes wonder whether originally a peile-tower was not situated here, a structure essentially of a fortified type with strong defensive facilities. The elms and oaks in the grounds of this derelict house were good trees, and although nearly all of them have now been felled, most of them were standing when I first had experience of the Old Moor House.

    That murder, or murders, have, in the past, been committed within the precincts of the policies, or in the house itself, is I think probable. Anyway such is the local belief. That gallows were once positioned within sight of the Old Moor House seems to be fairly good evidence that something of the sort did happen there. Since the gallows were removed there have been sudden deaths in the close proximity of the Old Moor House.

    My own original experience of this place was not a personal one. I suppose it could be described as second-hand, but that the story was reliable enough I have never doubted. The late Lord Ravensworth of Eslington first told me about the Old Moor House. Roy Ravensworth was full of fun. No one enjoyed a joke more than he did. He seemed always to be laughing, and there was seldom a moment when there was not a smile on his face. However, in spite of his jovial appearance and ways, I have no doubt myself that Roy was quite serious when he related to me his strange experience up on Rimside.

    Roy had been hunting with the West Percy Hounds. His sister was also out that day. A good fox had taken hounds some distance across the moors above Rothbury finally to ground in the extensive rocky fastness above Cragside overlooking the winding river Coquet. It was getting late and it was well-nigh impossible to dig the fox out, the hunt was called off and hounds and the various followers of the hunt had set off for home. Roy Ravensworth and his sister had quite a way to go from Cragside to Eslington. Riding together they made for the Devil's Causeway.

It was dusk by the time they reached the old stone bridge by the tumbled ruin of the Old Moor House. Here Roy's horse shied, tired as the mare was. The animal's fear seemed to transmit itself to his sister's mount. Both horses simply refused to cross the stone bridge. Every attempt was made to coax them over, but without success. Both animals got into a muck sweat, Finally Ravensworth and his sister had to make a detour on to the A.697 and so home. Roy was not himself scared or fearful in any way. Horses are known to shy and play up at all sorts of mundane things - a piece of blown paper, a tree trunk, a boulder, a pheasant or a couchant hare; the list of items likely to scare a horse, particularly in the gloaming, are innumerable. But that it was none of these things which frightened Roy's and his sister's horses that day Roy was himself certain.

"It was odd", he said. "But there it is".

Roy Ravensworth could be laconic at times. That there was something strange about the site where the Old Moor House once stood, Roy Ravensworth, I am sure, was convinced.

Not long after he told me this story I decided to go up to Rimside to investigate. It was before the era of myxomatosis and there were plenty of rabbits about up on the moors. I had with me two very sporting little Australian terriers which I used to breed at that time. I took them with me for a run on the hills. When I got to the clump of oaks and elms, which constitute the policies of what was once the Old Moor House, the two terriers who, up till then, had been particularly obstreperous suddenly quietened. They both came to heel and obviously did not like my going into the grove amongst the tumbled stones. Mattie, the old bitch, in particular, tucked her minute stump of a tail into her rump and even whined.

Both dogs were obviously miserable. I felt nothing. When I came away from the site of the Old Moor House Mattie and her younger companion became their usual energetic selves. When I told this story to a friend of mine he promptly scorned it, and to prove I was romancing he went up with his yellow labrador to investigate the phenomenon of the Old Moor House. His derision was even greater when he came back saying his dog behaved perfectly normally and there was nothing whatsoever uncanny about this place.

But this is not the end of the story, for some time later a local timber merchant purchased the standing trees about the Old Moor House. He put a gang of men on felling. The modern appliances of timber topping were assembled on the track by the clump of trees. A tractor, used to drag out the timber, in an attempt to pull out a fallen oak ran into trouble. The log began to roll sideways towards the ravine of the Wellhope Burn. The tree, lopped of its branches, had been chained to the tractor. The ground in parts hereabouts is boggy. The tractor began to slip and the weight of the trunk apparently started to topple the vehicle. The tractor came over to crush the driver to death. This accident did not enhance the local reputation of the Old Moor House.

Some months later a car coming along the A.697 crashed through the barrier of the viaduct over the Wellhope ravine, overturned, and the driver was killed. This spot is just below the Old Moor House and within sight of its remaining rubble. This sequence of events - the old reports of murder, the erstwhile existence of a gallows, the more recent deaths of a tractor driver and a motorist - has perhaps maintained the evil reputation of this place. It may be said to be accident-prone as some places are. There are dangerous spots on our roads which unfortunately have claimed many lives, there are perilous mountain climbs and treacherous shores where men and women have fallen to their deaths or been drowned. The Old Moor House may well be placed in such a category.

Recently I heard that the Old Moor House, or rather the bleak place where the house once stood, had been exorcised of its evil spirit by a religious person of some denomination or other which I have never been able to determine, nor have I been successful in finding out who the beneficent being was who performed the ceremony to do away with the alleged evil which was associated with this ruin.

This account, as written here, appeared in the magazine *Country Life* in 1968. On September 8th of the same year I received the following letter from the Reverend D. Brown of The Old Vicarage, South Charlton, Alnwick, Northumberland.

Here it is:

Dear Mr. Tegner,

I have recently read your article about the Old Moor House and feel that I must write and tell you of my own experiences there. About forty-five years ago I was staying with friends at a farm house in Longframlington and one morning decided to go for a ride on my bicycle round by the New Moor House to Rothbury. When I reached the point where the old coach road leaves the present highway about a mile and a half north of Longframlington, the old causeway covered with resilient turf looked so inviting that I decided to take this route instead of the present highway for I knew it met the main road just west by the present New Moor House.

All went well until I was approaching the old grove, where I got off my bicycle intending to investigate the ruins. Whilst I stood by the broken-down wall looking at the remains beyond, I was overcome by a feeling of sheer terror. Leaping on my cycle I pedalled towards the safety of the new road by the New Moor House. What remains to me as most extraordinary was,

(1) It was a fine and sunny day about noon.

(2) I thought I was the last person to have such an experience for I am far from nervous, and not in the least imaginative.

(3) Further I had had no previous details of this place so that my unusual experience came, as you might say "As a bolt from the blue".

Being thoroughly ashamed of my inexplicable fear I never mentioned this episode to a soul until I came across your article in

Country Life. Then I told my family and a few friends, believing that I had not been so susceptible as I had thought.

The Reverend D. Brown goes on to say in his letter that he had recently met a woman from Longframlington who had been acquainted with an old lady called Proudlock, who was over eighty when she died, and who had lived in the Old Moor House before it was torn down, as a child, with her father and mother. The somewhat vague account this old lady gave was that a party of horsemen and hounds were out hunting on the Moor when two men started a quarrel and remained behind. One of these men was found dead the next day. His companion, accused of murder, swore that he was innocent and was never condemned. Reverend Brown notes that this latter information would appear to be somewhat vague with no dates given. He has concluded his letter to me with these words:

"Anyway it is an evil place and I have never returned there.
Yours sincerely,
(Mins.) D. Brown."

Author's Note:

On Tuesday, 30th July, 1968, *The Journal*, of Newcastle, reported that one person had been killed and twenty six injured this year at the "New Inn" crossroads on the Wooler-Morpeth road. The "New Inn" is within sight of the Old Moor House and the site of the now defunct gallows.

THE LONE AIRMAN OF CHEVIOT
and
THE SPECTRE OF THE BOAR

The bald pate of old Cheviot itself - the namesake mountain of the range - is easily approached from the south from Wooler on the A.697 via the Harthope valley and then by Langleeford farm. From the north an asphalt track runs from

Kirknewton through Hethpool, and then parallel with the College Burn, to Southernknowe farm. Here the way forks to lead beside the tributary Lambden Burn to the croft of Dunsdale which lies due north of Cheviot and well within its shadow for most of the hours of daylight.

When I climb Cheviot I usually take the northern route. Somehow to me this way is more romantic, and the great, grim, dour ravine of Bezzil, above which the black ravens nest, has for me a peculiar fascination. I doubt whether the ultimate bowl of the Bezzil has ever seen the sunlight - even in mid-summer. It is a strange place this, this cleft in the hills, and not many people ever bother to go into the final depth of the gorge of Bezzil.

The Cheviot hills have, on many occasions, been described as a graveyard of planes. This is all too true, for many aeroplanes, over the years, have disappeared when presumed to be flying in this region. These lost machines were by no means all British, for the Germans, on their raids on Glasgow in the 1939-45 war, frequently took a course over the Cheviot range on their bombing missions - some of the German flying machines never got home; their graveyard is the Cheviot massif. During this period, when Britain was being struck from the air, the local Home Guard and some of the Cheviot shepherds were often out at nights searching for the bits and pieces.

There are men today who have engaged themselves in the grisly task of trying to trace and record all the planes which were believed to have fallen, at various times, amongst the high places of the British Isles. The Cheviots are one of them.

There were many R.A.F. stations, during the 1939-45 war, situated within close range of these hills below the Anglo-Scottish border. Acklington, Millfield by Ford, Morpeth and Eshott were amongst them. During the war planes from some of these aerodromes unfortunately ended up among the Cheviot Hills. Most of the casualties have, of course, been traced, but the lost German aircraft were not all easily accounted for. Post-war liaison with the Germans has resulted in an analysis of the Luftwaffe's losses but it is, of course, quite impossible for any investigation to determine, with any degree of accuracy, whether a plane has dropped into the sea or onto a sea of mountains. Crashed aircraft still occasionally crop up in the high places.

One day in June the urge to climb old Cheviot came upon me. I had heard a rumour that a pair of snowbuntings had staked a territory for themselves up on this high plateau, and that they had successfully brought off a clutch. This indeed was a rare ornithological event for the county if true and I was anxious to catch a glimpse of these lovely butterfly-like birds if I could. I decided to take my favourite route to the top along the ridge of Mid Hill. I could explore the summit and come down the flank of West Hill to the croft of Dunsdale. I drove up the College Valley road and parked my car, within sight of Dunsdale, on the close-cropped turf beside the asphalt strip. It was a fine day with the wind in the north. A nice cooling wind when climbing. There was a fair amount of cloud about, but as the eight o'clock forecast had been favourable, merely suggesting showers later in the day, I was optimistic. I took with me as I usually do, on my all-day excursions, my light Barbour oilskin. When I started to climb along the shepherd's track, which is well-trodden into the grey-grass of the lower slopes of Mid Hill, it was warm and I discarded my tweed jacket to carry it over my arm with my Barbour oilskin.

Once out of the shelter of the valley the north wind struck cold and before I was three quarters of the way up the path to the top of Cheviot a slight squall of rain had passed across the face of the Bezzil ravine. Sir Walter Scott once described the top of Cheviot itself as being as flat as a polo-ground. This is an exaggeration, for although the summit is flat it is also well-broken up in parts with little gullies, cups and numerous chocolate coloured peat hags.

By the time I got up to the top of Cheviot it was raining hard and blowing a lesser gale. Visibility was poor and as I braced myself against the wind and rain I knew that the prospect of seeing my snowbuntings was just about nil. I battled on intending to cut straight across the peak of Cheviot towards the sheep-track which meanders down West Hill to Dunsdale. Occasionally the rain dwindled and the sun would try to struggle through the cloud mass above.

    I tried to find some shelter where I could crouch to eat my now damp sandwiches. Finally I found some sort of cover beneath the lip of a bank of peat where the heather was overhung and beneath whose fronds the wet had not yet reached. I ate my meal quickly and emerged from my burrow with the intention of getting back to my car as speedily as I could. I had abandoned all hope of snowbuntings. As I came out into the open I heard the sound. It was an eerie, moaning cry which at times rose to a high-pitched scream as if someone were in great pain. It was an unusual cry and one that was somehow hardly human. No bird I knew of had a similar voice. The call of the curlew, the piping of golden plover and the remarkably versatile repertoire of the raven I was all well acquainted with. It was not a cry likely to be uttered by any of these birds, nor was it the utterance of any other bird or beast I knew of although the voice of an in-season vixen can be very strange at times when she raises her love-song to a falsetto screech. The cry came and went, rising and falling with the wind.

    I tried to locate its source and stood still to peer into the driving rain. I thought I could now hear the direction from which the noise came, and I made towards it. As I came to a small area of stunted heather in a sea of yellow-grass I could distinctly hear the piercing screech of something beyond the waving grass around me. Moving in the general direction of the sound I saw, almost completely buried in the dark peat, a mass of twisted metal some of which was red with rust. The screaming sound was now very penetrating. When I got to the wreckage of the aeroplane I realised at once what the eerie cry had been. It was the high-wind droning in a thin broken aluminium pipe which stuck out like a branch from the pile of debris. It looked to me like a hydraulic pipe or a petrol tube which had snapped when the machine had crashed. I began to examine the fragments which were scattered about with interest. This was old wreckage by the amount of rust about, and the extensive oxidisation present on the aluminium parts. There were also pieces of tubular metal, rather like those used in a bicycle frame, and a little dark green paint was still in evidence on this framework. Rightly or wrongly, I came to the conclusion up there on the top of Cheviot, that the remains of the broken flying machine I was examining was that of a fallen German plane which had possibly run into flak, been damaged and eventually run out, of petrol before being able to limp home.

It was while I was pondering about the past and the war in the air, in which I had participated in the R.A.F., mostly on the ground, that I saw the shadowy figure of a man, bent over slightly, as he faced the wind which had by now developed into a full gale. The form was clothed in what looked like a dark leather overall and the head, held low against the force of the gale, seemed to be covered in a sort of balaclava helmet. The man was moving fairly fast with a long stride. Now and then he seemed to stumble and then nearly fall on the rough going. I shouted at the top of my voice, but he obviously never heard me for he went on into the cloud wrack in the direction of Auchope Cairn. Try as I did I could not catch up with him, and I eventually lost sight of him in the driving rain. I found myself quite near the upper ridge of the West Hill and I was lucky enough to strike the sheep track fairly quickly.

I was now pretty damp, sodden would be a more accurate description. My one desire was to get back to the car. It was a long slippery scramble down the West Hill and I was very thankful when I saw the outbuildings of Dunsdale come into view. The rain and the wind had both decreased in strength and volume once I had reached a lower altitude. As I approached the house I saw the shepherd come out of a shed with his collie at heel. His close-fitting cap was on his head with its peak reversed; he wore what looked like an incredibly old and tar-blackened raincoat.

I went up to speak to him.

"Wild day", I said. He nodded, peering upwards towards the slopes of Cheviot above.

"Aye", he said. He did not seem to be a particularly talkative person.

"Been on the hill?" I asked.

"No", he said. "No need. Lambing's well past and the forecast was no good".

That was it. I wondered who the lone being was I had seen up there on the top of the bald pate of Old Cheviot.

On one occasion I was fortunate enough to glimpse a somewhat similar apparition. This was in the Scottish Highlands and I believe it is worth repeating here for the existence of these two spectres may well have a similar explanation.

The main road A.9 travels from Perth north into the wide strath of Spey. It is a popular road today with much heavy traffic. Past Pitlochry and Calvine the road enters open moorland and then the fringe of the extensive Cairngorm range of hills. Where the county boundary runs between Inverness-shire and Perthshire there are two conical hills on the west side of the road as you travel northwards. These are respectively the Sow of Atholl and the Boar of Bhadenoch. The Sow lies in Perthshire whilst the Boar is in Inverness-shire. The main railway line from Perth to Aviemore and Inverness passes beneath these two rounded hills. Beyond is the high ground with the mountains of Marcoanach and Geal Charn both over 3,000 feet. Between the Boar and these high hills there is a great corrie down which the Truim burn runs. The hill known as the Boar of Bhadenoch is part of the small deer forest of Druimachder or Drumochter as it is today more generally called. It was whilst I was stalking in Drumochter that I saw my second spectre.

One day, with Kennedy my stalker, I went into the corrie of Truim in search of a stag. From the usual spying point halfway along the valley we saw a suitable beast lying by itself halfway up the western flank of the Boar. It did not look as if it was going to be a difficult stalk. We decided to try for the stag. The weather conditions were good with a light breeze from the south-west and low clouds above which just touched the higher hills to the west. The sun would periodically break through bathing the glorious Highland glen in light.

Our plan was to follow the course of the Truim burn and then take one of its tributaries upwards towards where the stag lay. In doing this we would have ample cover and the wind would be right. I took the rifle from Kennedy, saw it was loaded and locked at safety. I put the rifle back in its case and told Kennedy to lead on. After crossing the Truim we started to climb along a little burn so as to get up towards the skyline of the Boar when we would be above the deer. It all worked perfectly. Once we had reached the desired altitude we proceeded parallel with the ridge of the Boar. In the meantime the cloud rack above us had come lower. Wisps of vapour now and again blotted out the contours of the hills around us. I was peering ahead to try and get a glimpse of the stag we were after when I realised we were being watched from above. Then I saw some movement against the backdrop of cloud. The man was huge. He seemed a monster, at least eight feet in height. He appeared to be standing on the ridge of the hill beyond. I turned to speak to Kennedy. He was staring at the apparition. There was a strange expression about his face. I took a couple of steps forward, the giant moved with me but he came no nearer. It was a rather uncanny experience. Suddenly the phantom disappeared as if it had climbed the ridge and gone over the skyline.

"Hikers?" I asked Kennedy, although I was pretty sure that there was unlikely to be hill-walkers along the ridge of the Boar for there are no footpaths there and it was unlikely to be a shepherd for Kennedy would have known if anyone was likely to be after the sheep during the time of the stalking.

"It's the Old Man" said Kennedy and then he added "We'll have no luck the day". He was right for when we got to where our stag should have been lying there was no sign of the deer, nor did we see another one that day.

That we glimpsed the phenomenon well-known as "The Spectre of the Boar" I have no doubt.

My theory for what it is worth, is this. By a trick of fleeting sunlight and mobile cloud wrack the shadow of one of us, Kennedy or myself, had been projected on to the mist along the ridge of the Boar of Bhadenoch. You can get the same sort of effect in an aeroplane when the sun is above the machine and there is a bed of cloud beneath. The clear cut shadow of the flying machine shows up distinctly as a dark silhouette on the sea of cloud below.

Could such an explanation also explain "The Lone Airman

of Cheviot?"

THE VARIOUS SILKIES

There was blood on his face and hands when I opened the front door of the house. He spoke in the quick way one does when one is shocked. He was apologising for being late. He had had a head-on crash with his car on Silky's Bridge he said. Fortunately no one was killed. It might have been a great deal worse. He told me who the other driver was. He happened to live in the village. Silky's Bridge is on the road between Stamfordham and Belsay. It was a notorious danger spot. There had been a number of accidents there and from what I have heard accidents which involved riders, and horses and carts, before the days of motor cars. Since this recent motor smash at Silky's Bridge the road over the Black Heddon burn has been widened and the approach ways to it straightened out. There have been fewer accidents since.

How the bridge came to be named after Silky is interesting. A woman who was always dressed in a rustling black silk dress was said to have lived in a squalid wooden hut on the bank of the river just below where the bridge goes over the burn. She was always known as Silky of Black Heddon for there were evidently other Silkies about in the north country at that time. There was one for example at Belsay who used to sit beneath a tree by the artificial lake near the Castle. This tree was known as Silky's Chair. Whether the Black Heddon Silky and the Belsay Silky were one and the same person it is impossible to say but it would seem likely as these two places in mid-Northumberland are only a few miles apart. These two characters were probably in their carnate days regarded as witches rather than spirits although the Black Heddon Silky certainly assumed a ghostly form after her death for her wraith is said to have appeared on various occasions by the bridge which spans the Black Heddon burn. Witches in the living days of the Silkies were regarded with dread, awe, hatred and suspicion.

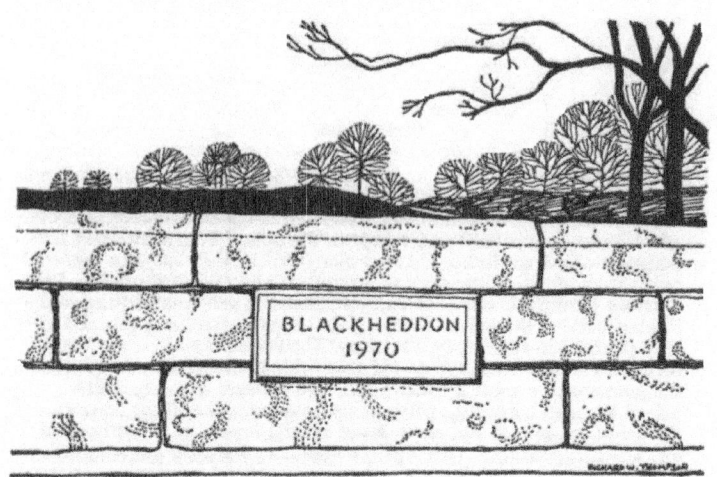

SILKY'S BRIDGE - BLACKHEDDON

Many of them, in all probability would have the "magical" powers of clairvoyance, soothsaying and telepathy. Some of them might well have been mediums as well. All in all they would have been a race apart. Eccentric beings and as such disciples of the Devil whose lot, in most cases, was an unenvious one. Thousands of witches, or female sorcerers as many of them were said to be, were the innocent victims of men's ignorance in the Middle Ages. After the passing of Silky of Black Heddon from this mortal sphere - no one has recorded how she died of natural causes, or by man's hand - her ghost was said to appear beside the little bridge named after her. Even during the present century I have met people who say that there is an aura, or something strange, about the bridge which spans the Black Heddon burn. People riding home from hunting have told me that their horses have shied and behaved abnormally when coming to this spot. Old records in the *Monthly Chronicle* of 1887 say that this Silky had a peculiar power over horses and on one occasion she was said to have been responsible for panicking a team of horses drawing a load of coals to a nearby farm, so that the animals bolted. Silky would appear to travellers on horseback and steal a ride on their pillion seats. Then she would rustle her clothing so as to frighten the animal when she would slip off and disappear. At other times she would stop horses in work or on the road immobilising them for as long as she wished. Silky seems, on occasions, to have been a mischievous sprite. Perhaps it is her ghost which still has its weirdly power over hunters?

All the ghosts or witches named Silky were said to have been dressed in satin or silk, a rustling, whispering material capable of giving off a sinister sound when its wearer moved. It is of interest to note that the so-called Banshee of Loch Nigdal and the Chappie of Houndswood were also silken ghosts. The other famous north-country Silky was Silky of Denton Hall. An old lady in black silk who occasionally showed herself in incarnate form in this old house. Thomas Doubleday has left a record of this apparition in *The Monthly Chronicle* (1887) and since then Eric Foster in his pamphlet *Tales of Northumbria* tells the story most excellently in much greater detail.

DENTON HALL - NEWCASTLE UPON TYNE

Denton Hall is an old manor house, to the west of Newcastle, constructed in part from the stones taken from the Roman Wall. As it had a reputation of being haunted by an old lady in rustling silk who would draw the curtains at night it was not easy to keep staff. In the distant past this place was believed to have been a sort of summer residence for the monks of Tynemouth Castle who would come there for a change of air from the coastal scene. Later bones were found in the policies which were believed to have been those of some of these religious personages. The house was named Denton after the Denton family who had acquired it in the time of Edward II. Subsequently it came into the ownership of the Erringtons.

When the Hall became haunted no one seems to know but that this house was, for a long time, the spiritual home of Silky seems certain for the locals were quite accustomed to view the wraith who became known as "Old Silky". Surprisingly, perhaps, this ghost seldom bothered the owners of Denton Hall, evidently preferring to show herself to strangers or visitors staying in the house. The owners of Denton, during the period of Silky's hauntings, appear to have been very hospitable people for it has been recorded that famous guests like Sir Joshua Reynolds, David Garrick and the waspish Dr. Johnson had all visited the Hall. The most spectacular appearance of "Old Silky" happened on the occasion when a young lady of wealth and fashion was staying as a guest in the house. The girl had attended a ball at the Old Assembly Rooms in Newcastle where the *haute monde* of the county and the city had put in an appearance. In the course of the evening the young lady had met a particularly charming and attractive young gentleman. It was a case of love at first sight. After midnight when the girl had returned to her room in the Hall and had locked her bedroom door, she sat in front of her mirror on the dressing-table in pleasant retrospect of the evening's doings. Suddenly something caught her eye and in an antique brocaded armchair she saw an old lady dressed in black silk with a number of large rings on her fingers. Her head was covered in a sort of mantilla, and her eyes were deep, keen and penetrating. "So you have been to the ball tonight? I can see how happy you are, but if you knew what is known to me you will not pursue this romance". The old lady appears to have said a lot more, quite a lecture in fact, on the iniquities of modern youth and the general wickedness of the times. "It is an age of glitter and gloss like the pearl in your hair" said Silky gesturing at the same time towards the mirror on the bureau. The young lady glanced towards the glass which held no reflection of the old crone and when she turned towards the chair it was empty. She heard the rustle of silk and the tread of feet on the way to the door but when she rose and went to the door she found it was still locked. Very naturally this young person was shocked but she appears to have taken her experience with a degree of equanimity for her day and age.

The footnote to this episode is that in the distant past, before Silky's warning and her appearance on this occasion, a lovely young girl was strangled in Denton Hall by her own sister but why or on what provocation no one seems to know. The house, however, for many years suffered from stories of a variety of manifestations, including the well known poltergeist phenomena of thumpings, levitations, dragging noises, footsteps *et alii* No wonder the various proprietors found it hard to keep staff.

MEG o' MELDON

Meg o' Meldon is our nearest ghost as she is said to haunt the precincts of the bridge, named after her, which spans the river Wansbeck to the west of the Meldon - Dyke Neuk road. Meg's Bridge is an attractive structure by the Old Mill which is now no longer in use.

Meg o' Meldon is no eldritch gnome or black-barbed crone; she is rather a stately ghost from a stately home. Who was Meg o' Meldon? Legend says that she was Margaret Selby, the daughter of William Selby, a wealthy money-lender from the City of Newcastle upon Tyne. W. Selby would probably be known as a banker today. Anyhow, William sounds as if he had been a very shrewd operator whose talents, in making and keeping money, Margaret appears to have inherited.

MEG'S BRIDGE - MELDON

Meg Selby married Sir William Fenwick of Wallington. Sir William would have been a good catch for a money-lender's daughter but Meg had presumably what William wanted, and that was cash. Included in Meg's dowry was said to be a heavy mortgage on the fair property of Meldon, the fettered inheritance of one Heron who seems to have been something of a good-looking, gay, young spark popular and well-liked by his neighbours. Heron, one reads between the lines, was generally hard-up. There is no tale of romance here between Meg and this handsome young man. One can only conclude that Margaret was not of the type who was likely to fall for good looks or charm. She appears to have been rather a close, calculating, shrewd female of no great physical attractions. The picture gallery at Seaton Delaval Hall used to have an old oil painting of Lady Fenwick with heavy ruff, Van Dyke sleeves, furbelow skirts and a Dutch type hat held down on a rather plain face by a big white bow.

Lady Fenwick had a number of children one of whom died for his King 250 years ago. Sir William predeceased his wife. (His battered effigy in sandstone still stands in Meldon Church.) Meg then foreclosed the Meldon mortgage when she proceeded to take an active part in managing and running the property. There is no doubt at all that Lady Fenwick, Meg o' Meldon, was a capable, at times ruthless, and a thoroughly good farmer and estate manager. To put it crudely she well knew how to turn a pretty penny. She would attend market in person. She knew a good beast when she saw one and could gauge a nice crop as well as any agriculturist in the land. Meg loved money and she seems to have done well enough for herself in increasing her initial dowry. Not unnaturally Lady Fenwick soon earned for herself the reputation of being miserly. People, behind her back, named her "Meg of the Moneybags". Heron of Meldon had been popular but poor. Meg was rich and envied.

As Meg grew older and richer she seems to have suffered from a form of possession dementia. She started to hoard her wealth, in the form mostly of gold coin, easily transported jewels and precious stones. In seeking for safe hiding places for her treasures she seems to have explored all sorts of likely and unlikely hiding places including almost certainly the supposed secret underground passage-way between Meldon and Hartington. Whether a subterranean causeway exists today or was ever in existence is I think doubtful. The banks of the Wansbeck, between the present Meg's Bridge and Hartington Hall, are in parts very precipitous and there are innumerable holes and crevices in the rock faces any of which could be thought to be the entrances or exits to non-existent passages.

"Meg of the Moneybags" began to wander here and there looking for likely safe hoarding spots; one cache was a bullock's hide full of gold coins which she had somehow lowered down a well on the Meldon estate. Meg o' Meldon, the present ghost, is believed to haunt this well.

After Meg's death a hind on the Meldon estate was said to have had a dream in which he saw Meg lowering her hoard of wealth down the well. Keeping this welcome vision to himself he crept out at midnight, equipped with chains and a grappling hook, to the cache. Aided by an unknown presence he nearly surfaced the loot when the chain broke and the now rotten bull's hide burst to release its contents into the slimy clay bottom of the well. The treasure has never since been recovered.

At Kirkhill, close by Hartington and now renamed Kirk Fenwick, there is a well and Kirkhill Hall, prior to its rebuilding, had its ghost, that of an old woman. Kirk Fenwick is some seven miles from Meldon. Meg o' Meldon was a wandering soul. Could this be Meg's well and the ghost that of old Moneybags? It is a thought. There are people still living in the neighbourhood who claim to have seen the ghost of an elderly female before Kirkhill became Kirk Fenwick.

Another of Meg's secret hiding places was evidently in the roof of Meldon school. Ceilings were strong and well built then and the hoard of gold stayed up above for some time until one day the uproarous rompings of the pupils shook down the plunder. The dominie came on the scene whilst his pupils were busy scrambling for the gold and silver coins.

"What is this you are striving for like a lot of eels in a basket?" was this learned man's enquiry.

The Spirit of Meg is said to be able to rest now as all her hoards have been discovered and distributed except the one in Meg's Well, which evidently she now no longer protects.*

Meg, I have been told, on more than one occasion is accompanied by a little white dog. Meg, like the Silkies, appears to have been of the wandering kind for her spectre has been reported as having been seen as far away along the Wansbeck Valley as Newminster Abbey where, with her small dog, she has been seen sitting on the old stone trough by the gothic archway. Hence presumably the Ghost of Newminster Abbey.

THE DEER KEEPER'S COTTAGE - MELDON

*The actual situation of Meg's well is a controversial one. I know of at least three alternatives. One to the south of Wansbeck, one to the north, and the old well by Hartington.

THE WHITE LADY OF CRESSWELL

There are a great many "white lady" ghosts, not only up here in the north but all over the country - all over the world in fact. The White Lady of Cresswell, like so many other white ladies, is certainly a pathetic figure as well as a very nebulous one. I have not yet met anyone who has seen her which is a little unusual because somehow or other most established ghosts have been seen, sensed or heard by someone. White ladies, of course, are so described because ectoplasm, of which ghosts consist, is a filmy, grey-white in colour. W. W. Tomlinson, in his *Comprehensive Guide to Northumberland* mentions the White Lady of Cresswell. The present old peile-tower at Cresswell is believed to be haunted by the spirit of a daughter of the house of Cresswell. From the tower's turret the young lady of Cresswell is said to have witnessed the brutal murder of her Danish lover, on the beach below the old lifeboat station, which is now a car-park, by her two brothers. She became insane, died and since then her spectre has frequented the scene of her life's tragedy, The Long Bay of Druridge, at the southern extremity of which is the village of Cresswell, is a quite well-haunted neighbourhood.

Some of the apparitions which are said to appear at times along the sand-dunes, beside the long bay of Druridge, have canine companions for it is said that big black hairy dogs occasionally accompany these spectres. It is extraordinary how spectral dogs always seem to be big, black brutes with bristling coats and luminous eyes. The dogs which travel with the Ghosts of Druridge have been described as large, black, hairy retrievers. They sound unusual animals, rather more like some of the sporting dogs used by our grandparents, such as the curly-coated retrievers and the dark Gordon setters, than the sporting dogs of today. These spirits only seem to put in an appearance during wild weather. When it is calm and mild the spectres are mostly quiescent.

Some say that these unearthly beings are the ghosts of a witch and her dog, whilst it has been suggested that the black woman of the dunes is the spiritual incarnation of one Bella Brown who became a local heroine after she had assisted in the rescue of a number of shipwrecked men. Heroines of the Northumberland coast have all been largely overshadowed, in the past, by the superlative Grace Darling whose feats of succour, farther up the coast on the Farne Islands, are now legendary. But Bella certainly appears to have done her bit, and a particularly good bit it seems to have been.

The girl Bella lived at Cresswell. A vessel went ashore on the rocks beyond Snab Point during a storm. Bella is said to have been the first person to have witnessed the disaster. She set off in the twilight fer the nearest lifeboat station which was then at Newbiggin-on-Sea farther along the coast. She struggled along the seashore in darkness, clambering over the dunes and wading waist-deep across swollen rivers, like the Lyne, which cuts through the dunes, until eventually she reached the moor of Newbiggin to call the lifeboat. Bella undoubtedly did a splendid job for it is recorded that most of the crew of the *Gustav*, a Swedish vessel, was saved. So far as I have been able to ascertain Bella, on her journey of mercy, was unaccompanied by any canine companion. So that those who claim that the Ghost of Druridge is Bella's have seemingly superimposed a dog upon the scene. Bella's, as ghosts go, is not an old one for the *Gustav* was wrecked on Snab Point somewhere in the mid-nineteenth century. Most ghosts have far older antecedents.

Bella was no witch but one of her alternate spectres is supposed to have been one. This local crone, for she appears to have been rather of an unbalanced type, lived at Widdrington, a village nearby. Sometimes this lady stayed out all night when she was believed to be sleeping out amongst the dunes always with her pet black dog.

The Witch of Widdrington however was not a victim of some dastardly deed; she was stranded by the tide on the rocks of

Cresswell –here she was accompanied by her black dog - was seeking mussels, In an attempt to get back to the beach she had tried to cross a shallow strip of water whilst the tide was coming in. She was drowned. Her black dog was never seen again, but when the witch appears nowadays, on a night of wild weather, the dog is always with her.

That the dunes can be eerie places at certain times of the year there is no doubt. I have frequently walked along this shore during the winter months in stormy weather. "A desolate coast" would be a proper description but, at the same time, in the spring and during the summer, on the occasional warm bright day, the dunes can be a most pleasant resort.

One day, in the month of November, I went to the sea for a walk along the beach. A succession of frosty nights had resulted in the sands becoming frozen down to the tide-line. For four miles, from the Cresswell rocks to the mouth of the River Coquet by Amble, a pale-grey strip of sand stretched northwards in one long graceful curve. Druridge Bay contains dangerous waters. At times there is a considerable undertow and the tidal rip can come in with incredible velocity. On this occasion the tide was well out and looking to the north and then the south I could not see a single soul in sight. I appeared to have the whole coast to myself. I was walking steadily in the direction of Coquet Isle off the sea-port of Amble. The island, with its white lighthouse tower and flat adjacent building, looked like a Mediterranean islet on which some rich man had built a luxurious villa. The sea was calm and the water a clear greenish colour which was also somewhat reminiscent of the sub-tropic seas.

As I walked the beach I saw, some distance in front of me and opposite the stretch of dunes by Druridge farm, a black lump on the shore. Focussing my binoculars on the lump I thought I saw it move. Boxes, barrels, fish-baskets and tree-trunks frequently get stranded on the sands of Druridge Bay. I once came upon a wounded grey seal on this strip of sand which refused to re-enter the sea when I tried to haul it back into its natural element. Through my field-glasses I saw the lump crawl a little way. I knew it was something alive, but it certainly was unlike a human form, and it looked like nothing I had ever seen before. The dog came into the focus of my binoculars from the direction of the dunes. It approached the lump then went off again. I was curious. It did not take me long to get up to the object for I was, by now, very intrigued.

When I got nearer I saw to my astonishment that the object I had seen through my glasses was, in fact, a human-being. She was an old woman, dressed entirely in black with a white scarf tied over her head. She was on her knees searching for little lumps of jet-black sea-coal which the receding tide had left stranded on the sands. The cloth of her dress was old and worn. It reminded me of the black box-cloth suits miners used to wear, in the past, on Sundays. She had on a pair of black gum-boots which seemed to be about the only modern things about her. When I got close to her she sat up from her culling. I do not know why, but she reminded me strikingly of James Abbot McNeill Whistler's oil painting *Portrait of the Artist's Mother*, which is in the Louvre, in Paris, and which shows an elderly lady all in black with a white lace cap reclining in a chair, only Whistler's mother was much more richly dressed.

When the woman started to speak, her black dog came across the sand at a lope from the sand dune area where he had certainly been having a fine time hunting the rabbits which used to swarm in this area in the days before myxomatosis.

"Lovely stuff", she said, and then she rattled the jute sack which was by her side and half-full of little nuggets of sea-washed coal.

"Hotter than any of your coal merchant's shale. Burn it in an open grate. Not many open grates left".

She bent over to pick up another piece of coal. I could not recognise her accent at all. It was quite unlike the speech used by the local folk. There was something remarkably aristocratic about her voice, and yet by her dress and deportment she was certainly no lady of culture. Knowing a little bit about sea-coal myself I observed causally that the recent tide appeared to have brought in some quite nice patches of this carboniferous stuff. Her dog, I noticed, was a regular mongrel. It looked like a cross between a greyhound and a sheepdog, very dark in colour, a real lurcher type. It had a badly undershot jaw and pale-grey eyes. I should not like to have met the animal suddenly on a dark night.

As the lady appeared to be very busy with her coal picking I did not dawdle but proceeded on my way northwards towards the mouth of the Coquet. When I looked back I saw the lady-in-black with her hound racing in front of her, disappearing into the sand-dunes. A sea-fret had commenced to come in off the bay so that a mist or cloud appeared to encompass the pair as they went out of my sight amongst the hillocks. I did not see her again or her hound.

I had one rather unusual meeting in this same locality. It was near the mouth of Hemscott Creek which runs out past the farm of that name into the North Sea half-way down the long bay. From Hauxley Point to Cresswell there is an almost continuous stretch of sand-dunes which varies in width from a few hundred yards to a quarter of a mile. The dunes, studded with marran grass, are like some great hairy necklace of the sea's. There are innumerable cups and hollows in this band of sand and many old concrete pill boxes, the relics of the 1939-45 war, most of which have now partially collapsed. It was in the month of April. The day at noon after several weeks of unpleasant cold weather had turned warm with the welcome foretaste of summer to come. In a well-favoured, sheltered hollow I saw a grey object move and then I realised it was a human form. The old man wore a sort of peakless tweed cap, a long overcoat down to his ankles with a piece of binder-twine tied around his waist instead of a belt. He was crouching low over a tiny fire surrounded by a number of small stones. On this impromptu hearth he had placed an old tin, which had once held some canned goods, and in which there was now a greyish nondescript liquid. All these details, at the time, must have impressed themselves on my mind but it was the old man's face surrounded by white bristly whiskers which was the greatest surprise. His grey piercing eyes and his smile could only be described as radiant. It was the face of an Isaiah.

THE LAMBTON WORM

The Lambton Worm is surely one of our most publicised local legends. A great deal has been written and spoken about this old myth, for myth it would certainly seem to be but like all imaginary accounts it has its interest which has grown rather than the reverse over the ages. The word "worm" appears to be a misleading description of this monster of the River Wear until one realises that the word "worm" is said to be a derivation of the old Norse *ormr* meaning a serpent or dragon. Surtees, Hogg and Scott were all at various times interested in the Worm and in the early 1800's Sir Cuthbert Sharpe, a friend of Robert Surtees, did a lot of research into this legend and its origin. His findings were duly published in the *Bishoprick Garland*. Mr. C.T. Oxley, in his little book *Strange Tales and Legends of the North Country*, gives a most excellent account of "The Lambton Worm". Oxley says that Surtees has left a note that when a young man he was shown at Lambton Castle a piece of what appeared to be akin to bull's hide, very old and dry. This, Surtees was told, was a piece of the worm's skin, killed long, long ago by an heir of Lambton.

I think, perhaps, it is because I have been a keen monster-hunter all my life that I have always had a particularly warm place in my heart for the Lambton Worm. Monsters have appeared over the ages in an enormous variety of shapes and forms. The Egyptian used to regard the crocodile as his dragon. The dweller on the coast had his leviathan or sea monster which may have been a whale, a porpoise or some still unknown variety of sea serpent. The Arabian in the desert regarded the poisonous snake as his particular monstrosity. Sir Walter Scott in his *Minstrelsy of the Scottish Border*, accounts for many legends of dragons by suggesting that in bygone days, before our country was drained and cleared of wood, large serpents may have infested British woods or morasses and taxed the powers of British champions. I believe that Surtees held similar opinions. These two certainly corresponded on the subject of the Lambton Worm. Lord Lindsay in his *Sketches of Christian Art* has written that the dragons of early tradition, whether aquatic or terrestrial, should not be regarded as wholly fabulous. In the former cases the race may be supposed to have perpetuated till the marshes or inland seas left by the deluge were dried up. Hence probably the legends of the many headed hydras, and so on. As regards the terrestrial variety the serpent may have been the dragon's predecessor.

LAMBTON WORM - CHESTER-LE-STREET

All this surely leads to our much more recent and current monsters like those of Loch Ness and Loch Morar, both in the county of Inverness-shire. I admit to having myself sought on occasion for these Highland monsters. One day by the shores of Loch Ness I thought for one moment that I had got a sighting. It was by Fort William and I had parked my car on the shore with a fine view over the loch. The day was bright and clear and there was scarcely a ripple on the water. As I sat gazing at the scene in front of me a slight breeze stirred so that the surface rippled. I first noticed the *thing* not more than twenty yards off shore. It was long, black and oily. It glistened in the sunlight. Knobs sprouted out of it like exaggerated nodules on an alligator. In the ruffled water the *thing* seemed to be gliding in towards the shore below where I had parked the car. My Zeiss binoculars soon showed me that I was looking at an old black log stripped of its branches. The next Highland monster I came across was in Loch Uaine in Glenmore's National Park. This Scottish lochan has a tradition of fairies about it for the Little Folk, who always wore garments of green, were accustomed to come down from the hills, where they dwelt, so as to wash their clothes in the clear, clean water, when the dye from their clothing left a stain in the loch. Loch Uaine is certainly unusually coloured, a sort of emerald green and so far as I can see there is no subterranean vegetation to account for its tint. It was a lovely mild day in mid-May when I last saw this little loch. There was a gentle wind which slightly stirred the water's surface. A sandpiper came skimming over the green depths towards me. The bird sheered when it saw the pink of my face against the long, rank heather above the miniature bay. Quickly a cold wind came down from Mam Suim, the mountain above, to churn up the green water of Loch Uaine. The little wavelets disclosed a whale-like form which appeared to be swimming out towards the centre of the narrow lochan. Once again it proved to be nothing but a log which at some distant day had been lured by the elements into the laundry site of the Little People.

My friend David James is surely the prime investigator and co-ordinator of the various sightings which have occurred of the Monster of Loch Ness. His recent report which appeared in *The Field* of 26th November, 1970, is certainly worth mentioning. In it he points out that in 1965, 1,500 visitors came to the Loch Ness Phenomena Investigation Bureau, mostly to mock; 1969, four years later, the number had risen to 32,000 and the majority came to question and learn. Over half a dozen books have now been written about the "monster" and the best perhaps is Mrs. Constance Whyte's *More than a Legend*, which deservedly has gone into three editions. Many illustrious names are now associated with the Loch Ness phenomena including such world-famed naturalists as Peter Scott and Richard Fitter. The American scientific world has recently become deeply involved and are now spending considerable sums of money on highly specialised equipment and machinery in order to solve the mystery. For mystery it still remains. Those who have seen the phenomena include surgeons, doctors, Benedictine monks, four ministers of religion, educationists and a Nobel prize winner. A pretty good galaxy. And so the evidence grows. Coincident with the Loch Ness sightings there have been others in such deep Scottish inland waters as Loch Morar where a number of reliable witnesses have recorded similar unusual appearances. In *The Times* of 25th November, 1970, a Mrs. Dora Metcalf of Otley, Yorkshire is reported as having given an account to a press conference, at the London Zoo, of several sightings of phenomena, similar to those of Loch Ness, in Loch Morar where she and her husband, a retired naval captain, had lived for a number of years. Mrs. Metcalf's account is one of twenty-seven in a report issued on this subject. Others claiming to have witnessed the Morar "monster" include Mr. Alexander Macdonnell, Mr. Charles Fishburne of Edinburgh University and Dr. Neil Bass, a marine biologist.

Well, so much for modern "monsters" or may we be permitted to call them "worms" in the sense that surely The Lambton Worm was, in its final form, a most monstrous thing.

One cannot but wonder whether the original Worm might not have been, in its embryo state, a sort of primitive culture which was to become eventually a far greater creature, just as the outcome of a crocodile's egg eventually grows into a reptile of several feet in length. Were the present monsters of Loch Ness and Loch Morar originally the sizes of small eels or lampreys as perhaps was that of the Lambton Worm?

The tale of the Worm has varied considerably over the years. There are quite a number of different versions of this delightful fairy story for such it surely is. The actual dates of the various happenings are also vague but that they all occurred during the time of the Crusades is evident as the hero of the story, John Lambton, "he that slew ye worm" was a Knight of Rhodes.

The park and old manor house of Lambton are situated to the north of Lumley a short distance from the modern London-Newcastle Motorway. The old castle was dismantled in 1797 when the manor house was built in its place. The story of the Worm however goes back some 400 years. John Lambton was evidently the youngest of five brothers four of whom died leaving him the heir. His father, who features largely in the story, must have led a very unhappy life, afflicted with grief, tormented with worry and the Worm. John Lambton in his youth appears to have been an unsatisfactory son who preferred hunting and fishing to estate management, religion or the so-called more serious aspects of life. One of his more dastardly deeds, it would seem, was his habit of fishing on Sundays. It was, in fact, whilst he was thus engaged that he caught the Worm. Fishing the Wear he had met with little success and was like so many of his brethren today cursing and bemoaning his lack of luck when he felt a mighty pull on his line. To his disappointment his captive proved to be only a small fish but of an unusual kind, this one having nine holes on either side of its head. Lambton threw the creature, in disgust, into a nearby well of clear water. When an old man passed to ask "What luck?" John turned and said "Why truly, I think I have caught the devil himself. Go and see," pointing at the same time towards the well. The old man confirmed Lambton's opinion of the strange appearance of his catch. The description of the vents by the side of the head lead one to conjecture whether this was a lamprey but the lamprey has only seven such openings. John's "odd" creature on the other hand might have been an eel as later it escaped from the well to go overland presumably into the Wear where it grew and grew until it assumed the proportions of a monster of considerable size and strength. Eels are well known to travel overland but in contradiction to this theory is the possibility that there may have been some subterranean passage between well and Wear. Eventually the Worm is said to have taken up its residence on an island in the river from which it periodically emerged to terrorise the countryside. So far as it is possible to ascertain the beast did not prey upon humans although its misdeeds did include a liking for lambs, harrying cattle and even frightening the peasantry. Eventually becoming extremely bold the Worm took up its lair near Lambton Castle where the old lord, father of John, was living. This caused further panic and to appease the monster, milk from nine cows was regularly kept in a stone trough for the Worm. Should, for any reason, its daily ration not appear, the Worm would twist its tail around the bole of a tree and lash the surrounding vegetation. Altogether the Worm appears to have been a nasty tempered animal.

During this time the old lord seems to have had to bear the brunt of the Worm's assaults and ravages, for long before this monster achieved maturity John Lambton, his sole surviving heir, had gone off to the wars. The wars, or Crusades, at this period of our history, would appear to have been a convenient *rendezvous* for love-lorn youths, errant young men, those seeking a fortune, the black sheep of various families as well as the deeply sincere and religious persons who thought all Saracens to be disciples of the Devil. Before going abroad John Lambton would have presumably got himself well equipped with a nice close-fitting coat of chain armour as the Saracens had a reputation for being expert swordsmen using very sharp weapons. That John knew something of body armour is later indicated.

The Crusaders appear to have done much for John Lambton for in due course this prodigal son returned to his old father and the family properties beside the Wear, a sober and a wiser man. During John's absence of seven years abroad a number of desultory attempts had been made by various persons to destroy the Worm but without any measure of success. The rumour was going around that the Worm if cut in half would join again. John's father was now old and decrepit and the estates in a poor way through neglect and the attentions of the Worm.

Young Lambton now wisely decided to visit the local sybil, which sounds a much nicer title than witch. This wise woman, who would probably have had clairvoyant powers and the ability to perform crude cures, levitations, and the like, had the courage to blame John Lambton for his early lapses from the straight and narrow and consequently for the present state of affairs at Lambton.

Because he was now a redeemed character the sybil undertook to help him rid his father's lands of their scourge. She advised this new Knight of Rhodes to have a special suit of armour constructed with several sharp cutting knives on its surface so that when the Worm would try and constrict the man it would cut itself to pieces.

The wise woman, however, made one stipulation namely that prior to combat John would have to make a solemn vow in the local chapel that if he killed the Worm he would then also kill the first living creature he would meet on his way home. If he did not comply with this request, then the sybil warned "No Lord of Lambton would die in his bed for nine generations". This "gypsy's warning" has its interest, in the spiritualistic sphere, for the question arises as to whether this wise woman believed in a form of re-incarnation and she therefore wished to avoid the Worm's re-creation by the immediate destruction of the nearest, most likely earthly potential "carrier" body.

Willing to comply with the sybil's request the young Lambton took his vows and with his father's agreement they then arranged between them, that in the event of John Lambton being successful in slaying the monster that he would sound his hunting horn when the old lord would immediately release one of his hunting hounds. The dog would then be the first creature to come to John who would immediately sacrifice the hound. John now went out girded for the fray, new armour and all. The Worm did its boa-constrictor act, was duly cut to pieces and the Wear ran red with blood. Meanwhile Lambton's father and his retinue up at the Castle waited anxiously for the sound of the horn. It came faintly over the breeze. The excitement was terrific; all thoughts of vows and stipulations were forgotten. John's father failed to release the hound, instead he rushed down to the Wear to embrace his hero son. He was the first living creature to be seen by John Lambton. To avoid patricide he sounded his horn once more. The hound appeared and was duly killed but the curse of the Lambtons was on them. Nine male members of the Lambton clan would surely die violent deaths in due succession. This prophesy would seem, at least, to have come partially true for John Lambton's son Robert was drowned at Newrig by the chapel where his father had taken his original vow. Sir William Lambton, a Colonel of Foot, was killed at Marston Moor, his son William died on the field of battle at Wakefield. Henry Lambton, who represented the ninth generation specified in the sybil's predictions died in his carriage crossing the new bridge of Lambton, on June 26th 1761, thus partially fulfilling the wise woman's prophesy.

There is an amusing footnote to the Worm's tale and the sybil's warning, General Lambton, Henry Lambton's brother, who succeeded him, is said to have kept a horse whip by his bedside so as to avoid any possibility of assault as he lay on his deathbed, a man of very great age.

THE POLLARD WORM

The Pollard Worm is no worm at all but a full-blooded male wild boar. This is hardly a ghost story but a very good yarn certainly worthy of the title of a legend. How the name of a worm came to be applied to that far from unattractive wild animal *Sus Scrofa*, the wild boar of the European Continent, is hard to say for even the old Norse description of *Ormr*, as meaning a serpent or dragon, hardly applies in this case. Serpents and dragons presumably are creepy, crawly creatures and not four-legged cloven-hoofed animals like wild pigs. But away with conjecture and back to this delightful legend, which is by no means as well known, up here in the north, as the much more publicised Lambton Worm.

The story starts in Co. Durham and ends in Northumberland. In the days of this old tale much of the two northern counties of Durham and Northumberland were well-wooded places. Such now extinct animals as wolves, beavers, lynxes, red deer stags, and wild boars would have been fairly common. The bear, however, would probably have been by then eliminated from the scene. No one knows exactly when these various wild animals ceased to inhabit the far north of England for there are but few records and some, at least, of those that exist cannot be entirely relied upon. Nonetheless in the days of the Pollards, a family of substance and standing, wild boars were evidently still about in the Palatinate and one old male in particular had begun to prove himself to be a considerable nuisance to the local peasantry. This wild pig was said to lair in the woodlands between the Wear and the Gaunless - a fair acreage of country. Old animals, especially if once wounded, are inclined to become savage. This applies, perhaps particularly, to beasts like lions and tigers, bull buffalos and old elephants - old boars can also become irritable in advanced age. The Pollard Worm, or wild boar, rapidly gained a reputation for ferocity. All sorts of devices were resorted to to destroy him. Many gallant hunters and knights sought his hide but in vain. The old pig stuck it out to continue his reign of terror. The legend says that several knights lost their lives in combat with the beast. This is highly unlikely or else they must have been pretty poor knights - a wild boar can wound a man but they have been very rarely known ever to have done a human being to death.

Things got so bad that, through the Bishop of Durham, the King issued a proclamation and offered a substantial reward "For he who would bring ye beast's head to Westminster". The Bishop himself backed up this order with a princely guerdon which my dictionary informs me is also a form of recompense.

The bait was there. Pollard decided to have it. This gentleman of yore appears to have been a good naturalist and expert hunter. He went into the forest where the boar laired and found its runs - wild boar, like so many other wild creatures, have their own ways and tracks through the woodlands. Pollard baited the ground in the vicinity of these runs with acorns - a favourite food of the wild pigs - and then built a hide in a tree to await the coming of the Worm. The old boar duly put in an appearance at dusk - their usual feeding time - and Pollard got his pig. With the coming of daylight the hunter cut off the boar's head and took out the tongue - still a great delicacy on the Continent. After his efforts he settled down for a brief nap. When he woke he found the boar's head had disappeared but the body was still there and he had the tongue in his wallet. The King's offer of a reward was for the head and not the tongue. Furious but undaunted Pollard now proceeded to Bishop Auckland and the Castle. Arriving in the evening as the gates were just closing and the Bishop was about to dine he requested an audience. The Bishop being a genial soul and knowing his Pollard he invited him in, accepted the bloody boar's tongue as evidence of the knight's successful hunting and told him his guerdon would be as much land as Pollard could encircle during the course of his Lord Bishop's forthcoming meal. Pollard, who appears to have been a gentleman very much on the ball, got his horse and then proceeded, at a gallop, to ride around Bishop Auckland. During the course of the prelate's meal he rode the boundaries of the whole of Auckland Castle and its grounds thus making the property his own. The Bishop, as well as being a genial soul, appears to have had a considerable sense of humour for he not only acceded to Pollard's claim and allowed him the freehold of the land but he astutely redeemed his own residence and all else on generous terms. Pollard's lands are still *in situ*. The Bishop made one stipulation that a Pollard would in future meet every Bishop of Durham upon the latter's arrival at Auckland Castle, and each had to present his Lord Bishop with a falchion, or broad, curved sword at the same time repeating "My Lord, I on behalf of myself, as well as several others, possessors of Pollard's lands, do humbly present your Lordship with this falchion at your first coming here, wherewith as the tradition goeth he slew of old a mighty boar which had done much harm to man and beast. And by performing this service we hold our lands".

The crest of the Pollard family became and remained an arm holding a broad, curved sword.

But what of the boar's head which had disappeared so mysteriously whilst Pollard slept? Here is where one of Northumberland's crafty old knights comes in, for the Lord of Mitford Castle, near Morpeth, happened to be en route through Co. Durham on his way to pay homage to his King at Westminster. He came upon the deeply slumbering Pollard and his recently slaughtered wild pighead neatly severed from the carcase. The temptation was too great. Mitford picked up the boar's head, slipped it across his saddle bow to canter on to London. Mitford, of course, was well aware of the King's reward. On presentation of his gory trophy this was accepted by the Sovereign as incontestable evidence that the courageous Mitford had successfully rid the northlands of a considerable menace. Mitford duly received the reward. As for Pollard, although he took his case to Court, he was never successful in his pleas. At any rate both of these astute gentlemen appear to have done pretty well for themselves out of the Wild Boar of the Gaunless.

N.B.
It is interesting to note that the coat of arms of the Mitfords of Mitford, near Morpeth, has as its crest a boar's head pierced by a sword held vertically.

THE WHITE LADY OF DUNSTANBURGH

The White Lady of Dunstanburgh is surely the most beautiful ghost in Northumberland. Her description in James Service's *Wandering Knight* conjures up in one's mind a pre-Raphaelite water colour, by Millais or Holman Hunt, of a girl with pale-pink cheeks and raven-black hair. This fair lady was certainly a beauty. Of all Northumberland's many castles Dunstanburgh - usually spelt in the past Dunstanborough - is the one I would select as the best positioned and most eldritch for the purpose of a haunting. My old friend, the late Sydney Moorhouse, who wrote a most excellent book, *Companion in Northumberland*, says:

"It is inconceivable that such a castle should not have its legend of the supernatural. Its very position has suggested a multitude of stories the most famous being that of the imprisoned beauty".

Those of us who have lived within the two northern counties and who have not visited Dunstanburgh Castle have missed something rare, for Dunstanburgh is a ruin of remarkable character. Once you have seen Dunstanburgh you never forget it.

The castle stands out in all its stark grandeur against a superb seascape. To the west is the distant Cheviot range whilst to the east there is the seemingly empty, endless North Sea. The water is intensely clear being quite free, along this part of the Northumbrian coast, of any serious pollution from the industrialised areas. At times, and according to the mood of the weather, the sea changes colour from pale green to a deep indigo. The downs of close-cropped, springy turf, around the castle, come right down to the brief stony beach. To walk on this sward is almost an exciting sensation. I have never encountered pleasanter ambulation. The best time of year in which to visit Dunstanburgh is, I think, the spring; a mild day in May with a light breeze from the south-west - an off-shore breeze which leaves the sea quiet by the stone-strewn beaches. Dunstanburgh is best viewed against a typical Northumbrian sky - lambs-wool clouds bunched and again pulled out in fleecy whiteness against a deep-blue vault. The castle is also immensely impressive on a wild day of winter weather or on a day of warm summer sunshine. I have walked the short distance from Craster to the castle on many a day of wind and rain as well as those of nigh-tropic weather.

The usual approach to Dunstanburgh is via the fishing village of Craster, famed for its kippers and salmon. Cars are not allowed past the end of the village. This is a good thing for otherwise the lovely natural downland, beside the seashore, would certainly quickly become covered with blown filth and litter from hundreds of parked vehicles. The short walk to the castle from the Craster village road-end can be an ornithological delight. Sanderling, dunlin, turnstone and purple sandpipers, a flight of pied oystercatchers, redshank, and curlew, whilst out at sea there will be the eiders and the big blackbacked gulls. A cormorant may show itself and if you are lucky, a lovely, jaunty red-throated diver with its upturned beak like some aquatic Johnny-Head-in-the-Air. Once up at the castle the views all around are simply immense. There can be few coastal scenes like them in the British Isles. Below the walls of the old ruined fortress are the extensive gorse covers in which the phantom fox, told of in *The Shadow on the Moor*, led Black Tom the huntsman to his gruesome grave.

To the east the walls of the castle and its surrounding grounds fall sheer into the North Sea. The cliffs are the favourite breeding grounds of innumerable fulmar petrels. There is a rather narrow frightening cove below Dunstanburgh's ramparts, known as the Rumbling Churn, where ships of war were once said to harbour but as this narrow gut always seems to be in a turmoil it certainly does not look like a safe shelter for any sea-going vessel. Dunstanburgh castle is today in the keeping of the Department of the Environment and they have done their work of preservation well.

But to the story of Dunstanburgh's White Lady whose frail ghost is said to be seen by the stark turrets of the old castle. It is a romantic tale with a number of versions nearly all told in a form of verse which has been given the name of a metrical legend. The editor of these verses, one James Service, has had them printed, with suitable editorial comments, in a little booklet entitled *Metrical Legends of Northumberland*. This delightful work was published by the old printing house of William Davison of Alnwick in 1834. It is a rarity now.

Service's collected poems nearly all deal with one he names The Wandering Knight.

Sir Guy, the Wandering Knight, just as John Lambton the Worm Slayer, had done his bit in the Mediaeval Christian wars to recover the Holy Land. The Crusades lasted for nearly 200 years. The first crusade was in 1096 whilst the last, under Edward I, was undertaken in 1270. It is said that in 1096 not less than 6,000,000 souls were in motion towards Palestine. William of Malmesbury has left a record that "The Welshman left his hunting, the Scotsman his fellowship with vermin, the Dane his drinking party and the Norwegian his raw fish". Six million souls is surely a huge exaggeration; nevertheless great hordes under such leaders as Walter the Penniless, Peter the Hermit, Gottschalk the Priest, did start off for the Holy Land, many of them never to return. Like all warriors of the Crusades, Sir Guy came back with no victory accomplished but certainly a changed and perhaps a disillusioned man.

One wild, windy night when the full moon was overcast and Dunstanburgh's castellated turrets stood out against a sullen sky, Sir Guy chanced to ride beside the sea on the turf track which now so many tourists tread. Lights shone from the upper grills of the great studded portals. He cantered his charger up to the drawbridge to find to his amazement that the bridge was down and the massive doors of the castle began to swing open.

A voice spoke whilst at the same time a nebulous human arm appeared above the portals.

> "A glimmering light appearing
> The portal's gloom dispelled;
> And a shadowy hand uprearing
> A lamp, the knight beheld
> A hand and arm alone -
> Nor form nor face was there
> All ghostly white they shone
> By the dim lamp's fitful glare!
> Slow moved ahead the spectral hand"

To the accompaniment of a peel of monastic bells and the sound of shrieks and screams like unto those of some abandoned soul, Sir Guy was commanded to enter. Leaving his charger by the gate he came to a magnificent chamber draped in brocades and flower-patterned tapestry. Glistening marble pillars interspersed with statues of knights carved from alabaster and bronze horses stood together whilst as the centre piece a beautiful woman reclined encased in a great crystal globe poised on a stand of intricately carved pink coral. The floor was of the finest mosaic and bright flaming chandeliers lit the scene.

The Wandering Knight's gaze was riveted to the imprisoned lady, her tresses long and raven and her breasts like perfect peaches. The disembodied voice spoke once more whilst the phosphorescent arm offered a choice of golden horn or sword; the chosen instruments for the release of the imprisoned maiden.

Sir Guy chose the horn - his choice was wrong - the vision vanished. The choice of symbol is the moral of this poem, Sir Guy in choosing the horn lacked personal valour for he would be summoning assistance with its blast. The selection of the sword would have signified his own bravery as he would then have sought to free the maiden by his own might.

The disillusioned knight eventually came to his senses outside the castle walls - drenched to the skin and icy cold.

Now on dark wintery nights of gale and hail the pale white ghost of the White Lady still appears awaiting some Wandering Knight whose choice will surely be the sword and not the horn.

Some say that the spirit of poor Sir Guy, under similar climatic conditions, persists in haunting the surroundings of the castle seeking in vain for his lovely lady.

THE GHOSTLY BRIDAL OF FEATHERSTONEHAUGH

This is a good, gruesome, ghost story located in the south-west of Northumberland, the district, Herbert Honeyman points out in his book on *Northumberland*, which is frequented by a number of hauntings. Honeyman's Pinkie's Cleugh, mentioned in a previous chapter, is the Pinkyn Cleugh of the Ghostly Bridal. Featherstone Castle the scene of the story is situated on the South Tyne between Haltwhistle and Alston. *The Monthly Chronicle* of 1888 gives a full and detailed account of this good ghost story.

One Abigail, the lovely and only daughter of an early Baron Featherstonehaugh, was her father's pride and joy. Unfortunately Abi's nubile affections were centred on a gentleman, described as "A young gallant of somewhat doubtful lineage, who boasted himself, indeed, to be of gentle birth, as perhaps he was, but whose means of supporting the dignity he assumed was doubtful, as he had no landed estate, honest profession, or known settled allowance".

So says *The Monthly Chronicle*. The account of this somewhat attractive young rascal continues:

"He lived well, was handsome, and well versed in all the niceties, hunting, singing and dancing".

One can easily imagine the mutual attraction of these two young people for Abigail had wealth, a draw for any indigent young gallant whilst her boy-friend had good looks and charm. That the affection of this handsome young man for the Baron's daughter went deep there is no doubt for subsequent events more than indicate this. The Baron favoured, for his daughter's hand, "a man of equal birth and fortune with his own and one of exceptionally good character". This was the situation when it became obvious that an elopement or runaway marriage between Abigail and her young lover began to appear very imminent.

Baron Featherstonehaugh decides to take matters into his own hands. He prevails upon his daughter to take his own choice of bridegroom in marriage. No details are given of the old Baron's means of coercion. The marriage is immediately accelerated. Great preparations are made for a magnificent ceremony. Guests are invited from far and wide. Musicians and entertainers are engaged. Wine, ale and exotic foods are prepared. Ail in all Baron Featherstonehaugh does not appear to have stinted himself in any way over the lavish arrangements for his beloved daughter's nuptials. The Priest of Haltwhistle is to officiate.

All goes according to plan and there appears no hitch of any sort - no elopement or failure of the bride to appear. The two are joined together in Holy Matrimony - the knot is duly tied in public view. The Baron must have sighed his relief but he did not remain content for long as tragedy was on its swift way.

Towards evening when many of the guests had gone and the merrymaking and feasting quietened it was decided that the bridal party accompanied by a few select friends would now take a little relaxation by riding the bounds of the Featherstone property, for there was to be that same evening another feast at which the Baronial tenants and the peasantry would be present.

Promising to be back in good time for the evening's festivities the bridal party move off, never to return in carnate form. The tenantry arrive but there is no sign of bride or groom or any of their attendants. The Baron becomes anxious but decides to let the festivities continue. He sends out messengers who return without news. The tension within the castle and Baron Featherstonehaugh's own nerve-racking anxiety, and apprehension are well described in *The Chronicle's* account of this evening of fear. By midnight the old man is frantic. Those of the diners who are left are dismissed, he sends the household servants off to their quarters. He sits alone in the great, baronial banqueting hall.

Suddenly he hears the sound of horses' hooves on the unmetalled road outside the walls of his castle. The drawbridge drops of its own accord. The bridal cavalcade returns led by Abigail and her unloved bridegroom. They dismount in the court and proceed to the banqueting hall. The old Baron sees the married pair and their entourage take their seats. Their pallor is ashen, their eyes staring as if in death, ghastly wounds gape, there is blood everywhere and horror in all the faces as if they had all present been done to some brutal death. The Baron makes, on his head the sign of the Cross. A rushing wind sounds and the phantom party is no more.

In the dawn the servants come to sweep the banqueting hall and to clean up after the revels of the previous night. They find the old Baron in a stupor from which he is roused with difftculty. He has gone raving mad.

The story goes on to tell that the wedding party were ambushed in a ravine named Pinkyn Cleugh by a gang led by Abigail's rejected suitor. Both sides die to a man. People since then are said to avoid the precincts of Pinkyn Cleugh towards evening for fear of the spirits of the ghostly bridal and its attackers who now haunt this place.

Like so many another ancient legend this tale of the Ghostly Bridal has been repeated with several variations. For the description given briefly here I have relied on William Pattison's account in *Richardson's Local Historian's Table Book* from which *The Monthly Chronicle* seems also to have drawn and as the editor of this monthly magazine of December 1888 comments:

"Where our account differs from that (of Pattison) we have

followed what we believe to be good oral authorities, who may, however, have been like Sir Walter Scott's grandmother - awful liars".

THE GREY MAN OF BELLISTER

And now from White Ladies and Ghostly Bridals to Grey Men. Whether the Grey Man of Bellister was so named because the final, earthly aspect of his ghost was that colour or because he happened to be a very old man when he met his sudden, brutal end has never been explained. I have mainly drawn on two sources for my information about the Grey Man. First from our old friend William Pattison of Bishopwearmouth who in turn related this yarn for the benefit of Richardson's *Local Historian's Table Book* and secondly from the vivid account of these happenings which appears in Eric Forster's *Weird Tales of Northumbria*. Forster has described the events, which took place at Bellister Castle on the evening of the Grey Man's decease, with his usual journalistic flair. He entitles his story "The Ghostly Minstrel of Bellister".

Pedlars and minstrels were important individuals during mediaeval times for not only did the one supply necessary goods and chattels but the other provided equally welcome entertainment. The former would probably have paid for his lodgings in goods whilst the latter would sing for his supper. Both pedlars and minstrels were also welcome not only for their commercial, or entertainment, value but because in these early days of poor communications they would be able to bring news of the doings of the outer world.

As has already been stated and as will be seen later in this book there are many ghosts of pedlars but perhaps not so many of minstrels. Pedlars were, on the whole, likely to have been better endowed with this world's material goods than minstrels and hence they were better worth murdering. In certain observations of the occult the theory has been put forward that sudden death or murder will result in a man's departed spirit becoming earth-bound. Hence presumably the frequent apparitions one hears about which are the ghosts of murdered people. At least, in the days of yore, a good many pedlars appear to have come to some pretty sticky ends. Minstrels, because they were hardly worth the killing, seem to have come off better.

Old Bellister Castle is situated near Haltwhistle in the South Tyne valley; one of Northumberland's most ghost haunted areas. Down to Elizabethan times Bellister was the seat of a younger branch of the Blenkinsopps of Blenkinsopp Castle whose heir was entitled to the distinction of baron by courtesy. It was presumably during this period that the ghost of the Grey Man came into being.

Pattison of Bishopwearmouth gives a detailed description of the then ruling baron's character. A suspicious man, who evidently suffered from a form of persecution mania, Baron Bellister always believed that others were envious of his wealth and position and that certain parties were prepared to rob him and even take over his properties. He appears to have been fearful of spies in particular and it was largely because of his espionage phobia that the old minstrel came so suddenly to his gruesome end. Bellister was a wealthy man owning many acres of good farmland. He was evidently fond of sport and hunting for he kept a private pack of hounds. He had a large retinue of servants. He did himself well and his table was usually laden with succulent viands, good ale and wine. The Castle would have been a popular stop-over spot for itinerant people - pedlars and minstrels.

One evening after a day of foul weather, an old grey haired man came to Bellister's portals to seek shelter for the night. He said he was a wandering minstrel and that he was quite prepared to entertain the household in return for a bed and a meal. He was invited in. The entertainer's repertoire does not appear to have been of high quality. His voice was feeble and at times cracked with age. However, he seems to have done his best and, as was usual with the profession, he laid on a good measure of fulsome praise about the splendid character and fine qualities of his host of the night. Perhaps the wandering musician laid it on too thick? Anyway, the Baron became his usual suspicious self and when the minstrel excused himself on account of his fatigue and his advanced years to retire early, the Baron Bellister became even more suspicious. Towards midnight he had worked himself up into a state of high tension. He was convinced that the visitor, within the precincts of his castle, was probably a spy who had come, to use a modern expression, "to case the joint".

Baron Bellister could not rest. He sent one of his minions to rouse the minstrel. One can imagine the bold Baron's reactions when he was told that the minstrel had fled. There was only one thing for it - lay on the hounds. Quickly assembling a posse of mounted men Bellister goes to his kennels and with the aid of a bedsheet which the minstrel had touched he puts his bloodhounds on the drag. Towards dawn hounds come up to their quarry in a thicket of silver birch by the banks of the South Tyne. The poor, pathetic old minstrel was broken up like a hunted fox. One can only hope his death was swift as is nearly always that of a fox. When the riders eventually arrived at the kill Bellister appears to have been filled with remorse. He became increasingly morose, always haunted by the memory of the man whom he had so brutally done to death. The ghost of the little, old, grey man followed him in the daylight and the darkness. It was not long before the baron went to his own grave. It appears as if his guilty conscience killed him. And now the phantom form of the little grey minstrel still appears at times in the neighbourhood of the castle or along the banks of the South Tyne where the silver birches grow.

THE WHITE LADY OF BLENKINSOPP

Here is another White Lady; somehow you cannot get away from them up here in the north. They almost seem to swarm. The White Lady of Blenkinsopp is of particular interest to me because I know a man who has seen her. He is no romantic, nor is he credulous or psychic. He is one prominent in the City of Newcastle's book business. I met him one morning in Grey Street whilst I was engaged in preparing this book. I thought he might be able to help me trace some records of local ghosts and hauntings. In the course of conversation I asked him, as I have asked a lot of other people, whether he believed in ghosts. I expected to get a negative reply. I was quite astonished when this gentleman of complete integrity said:

"Yes, I've seen The White Lady of Blenkinsopp"

"What did you do?" I asked

"Run like hell" was the terse reply.

Well there it is. It was one of my better moments whilst researching the local occult.

The White Lady of Blenkinsopp is a queer anomaly for in carnate form she was a lady of colour if not exactly a blackamoor. Lady Blenship was brought back to this country from far foreign parts by her husband, one of those many Crusaders who seem to have set off periodically from our two northern counties during mediaeval days in search of something or other. This particular Knight of Rhodes appears to have been one of the adventurer types who took to the Crusades primarily in search of treasure, or more prosaically, loot. Bryan Blenship, as he was named, when he set off on his foreign adventures seems to have been one of those "Get-rich-quick" types which one still reads of in the financial columns of our daily newspapers. Bryan found no hordes of jewels or gold bullion but he did pick up a wealthy heiress whose dowry was stated to have taken four men to carry and it was not lead. The lady in question appears to have been a sensible sort who had no intention of handing over her personal fortune to her bold knight, lover and husband. She seems to have kept a close eye on her dot. Although his wife's wealth made Bryan one of the richest men in Northumberland, neither his wife nor himself were able to enjoy their fortune. It was not long after their home-coming - Lady Blenship with her own personal retinue of dark-coloured servitors - that husband and wife began to quarrel. Then suddenly both disappeared from the Northumbrian scene, but not before her ladyship had managed to conceal her chest of gold. Where had she concealed it? The general belief appears to have been that it had gone, chest and all, into some concealed dungeon below the castle itself. It was not until a century or more later that some sort of clue appeared concerning the whereabouts of this wealthy, dusky heiress's horde.

Blenkinsopp Castle, situated halfway between Haltwhistle and Greenhead, was left unoccupied. It started to fall into ruins until an agricultural worker and his wife and child took to occupying a part of the old buildings. The original castle was believed to have been re-erected about 1339 with stones taken from the Roman Wall. This was the seat of the ancient family of Blenkinsopp. Later one Thomas de Blenkinsopp got a licence to fortify his mansion against the Scots. But by the time the hind and his family took over, what remained of the seat was pretty shaky. All the glory had well and truly departed.

This couple seems to have been somewhat unusual for their age for father and mother had a room to themselves whilst their little son had his own sleeping quarters. Most families of this sort, a hundred years or so ago, would have huddled together in one place for their slumbers. One night the boy awoke shrieking "The White Lady, the White Lady".

Mother and father quickly went to their child to see what was the matter and to quieten him. They told the boy he had had a bad dream and to go to sleep again. The same thing happened the next night and the night after that. The boy described the White Lady as leaning over his bed and repeating that she had much treasure and she wanted to show the child where it lay. On one of these visits the Lady had become so persistent that she had tried to lift the youngster off the bed. The hind and his wife then took the boy into their own room to sleep. The White Lady never seems to have appeared to the lad, or his parents, again. This looks like the not unusual case of an imaginative child having nightmares. The White Lady of Blenkinsopp is an altogether unsatisfactory ghost. There is so little material evidence about her except, perhaps, her appearance to my friend in the book trade, but then he ran away.

Eventually the structure of Blenkinsopp got so dilapidated that it was condemned for human usage. A farmer decided to adapt parts of it for a steading for his cattle. Whilst at work on this project the workmen came upon a well or dungeon within the precincts of the castle. It was convenient in the days of old for any fortified place to have its own internal supply of nice, clean, cold water especially should it ever become beleaguered. The man organising the re-construction does not appear to have been at all interested in the well. He had probably never heard of any buried treasure. One can almost hear some old private-enterprise contractor shouting at his workmen to "Leave that muckin' well alone and get crackin' with the concrete!"

William Patterson, who is quoted in Richardson's *Table Book*, mentions that the last time he saw the hole, some boys were throwing stones down into it so as to listen to their long-delayed "plop" as they hit the water a long, long way down.

THE SPECTRE OF HAUGHTON CASTLE

Haughton Castle on the banks of the North Tyne, opposite to the charming Northumbrian village of Barrasford, is an impressive pile. The castle is a good example of the fourteenth century tower houses which used to rank as castles. It is inhabited today and parts of it have been modernised. A small ferry once operated between Haughton Castle and Barrasford but this public service has now been discontinued. Across the river from Haughton was one of the country's best trout fisheries but this too is now defunct.

The story of the Spectre is a good one and it sounds probable. The characters involved appear true to life and the action realistic. The aftermath and the subsequent spiritualistic happenings have an aura of reality about them.

It is necessary to go some way back in history to the actual time of creation of this ghost but not so far as many another north country spectre. It all happened during the period of the moss-troopers, border-reivers, Scots raiders, *et al*. At this time the Lord of Haughton was one Sir John de Widdrington. He was a good and upright man, conscientious, energetic and peaceful who was always anxious to do what he could to quell the unruly elements in the North Tyne and Border neighbourhood. Sir John has been described as a learned clerkly man though as gallant a knight as any in the North Country.

Whilst Sir John de Widdrington ruled at Haughton, a contemporary Lord Dacre of Gilsland was appointed Lord Warden of the Marches. The task of Lord Warden would appear to have been a pretty unenvious one. He had to try and quell the unruly elements, and they were far from few, up here at this time. There were a number of notorious trouble makers like the Armstrongs, Kerrs, Elliotts, Scotts and the Graemes, not to mention the Scotsmen over the border as well. Lord Dacre, unlike the Lord of Haughton, appears to have been a somewhat weak character, quite the wrong type to have had to handle a horde of rascals.

Dacre soon got himself into the hands of the unruly elements. He was quickly suspected of taking bribes and conducting extortion rackets. He was said to be hand-in-hand with such picturesque characters as Johnnie o' Gilnockie, Wat o' Harden and Kinmont Wullie. Worse still his lordship began a clandestine affair with a female of the Armstrong clan, one Helen, a raven-haired beauty known as Dark-eyed Nelly. Helen Armstrong was the sister of the Armstrong who was the leader of his family troop of reivers. Things got worse and worse so that the local landed proprietors were forced to form an association to protect their rights and to report Lord Dacre's misbehaviours to the King.

Sir John de Widdrington was their chosen envoy. It so happened that conveniently Lord Cardinal Wolsey was visiting York. It was therefore decided that Widdrington with two other representatives of the landowners association should visit York and present their case to Wolsey. On the night before the delegation was due to leave for York some of Sir John's retainers captured a reiver thieving cattle in the North Tyne meadows. The Lord of Haughton immediately had this man put in the dungeons to cool off. Next morning Sir John set off with his deputation for York. After two days steady riding, on their arrival in the city, Sir John suddenly realised that he had with him the key to the dungeon and worse still that he had left no instructions with his staff to either feed or water his prisoner. In a fearful state of perturbation he immediately turned round to gallop home. By the time he got to Durham he had killed one horse. He easily obtained another to hasten full speed northwards. Forty eight hours later he was at Haughton Castle. On asking his retainers, "How fared the prisoner?" he was told that the man had made a lot of noise and then he had started screaming but finally he had quietened till no more was to be heard from his cell. Unlocking the dungeon the unfortunate moss-trooper was found dead. In due course the disembodied spirit of this unknown reiver came to haunt Haughton. In the dead of night when the cold winds blew down the North Tyne valley from the north, the sounds of this demented creature's cries and moans rang through the night. No servants would stay. Things came to such a pass that something had to be done. The Rector of Simonburn was called in to exorcise the ghost. This he appears to have done most effectively with a "black-lettered" bible which remained, after the exorcism ceremony, within the castle walls. The haunting cries of the reiver quietened, his ghost was laid. The curious thing is that later when this bible was removed and sent to London for re-binding the moss-trooper's voice of agony was heard once more, moaning and piteously wailing. The bible was hastily brought back from the London book-binders and replaced in Haughton Castle since when the reiver's spirit is said to have remained quiescent.

POLTERGEISTS AT CALLALY CASTLE
and
THE WITCH OF EDLINGHAM

Callaly and Edlingham, as the crow is said to fly and seldom does, are in a straight line four miles apart. Both buildings lie in hollows so that you cannot see them from one or the other.

Edlingham is today a complete but nevertheless attractive ruin. Callaly is a dignified square-built residence in splendid condition. It is inhabited and is redolent of the days of gracious living. At certain times of the year Callaly is open to the public. Edlingham lies in fields beside the now disused railway line from Alnwick to Wooler. This old railroad once travelled through some of the loveliest countryside in Northumberland. Callaly is situated in well-kept park-like lands. Callaly's supernatural phenomenon would seem to have been some form of poltergeist. Edlingham's, on the other hand, was a straightforward, old-fashioned witch of quite remarkable character.

A poltergeist my dictionary says is a noisy mischievious spirit. There is more to poltergeists and poltergeistism, if I may so coin the word, than that. Spiritualists now know a lot about the mischievousness of poltergeists. There is an enormous literature on the subject of spirit materializations, apports, levitations, and the like and it must be admitted that some of these so-called spiritual manifestations have been faked but on the other hand there is much evidence to show that the demonstrations of the poltergeist have close supernatural associations. Take apports for example. These are material things like jars, ironware and nails which have been made by mediums to appear out of thin air. There used to be a museum of apports in Budapest run by a certain rich gentleman, doctor and chemist, by the rather unusual name of Dr. Chengery Pap. Pap was a sincere confirmed spiritualist. To get some idea of what mediums and poltergeists can do I would refer the reader to an excellent, recent Pan paperback by Douglas Hunt entitled *Exploring the Occult*. It makes good reading and it does more, for it makes one think.

It is not easy from the few records available to say whether Callaly's "ghost" was the work of poltergeists or of a fake or fakers. But here is the story, so that you may be able to judge for yourself.

When the present residence was built at Callaly the original site selected was said to have been upon the heights above the beautiful Vale of Whittingham but every time an attempt was made to start the foundations they were found to have been torn down or otherwise disturbed during the night. Noises emanated from the site of the building and the stones carried up for its construction were hurled about. A plan was made to catch the poltergeists. A party sat up by the cleared space for the house but nothing happened until about one o'clock in the morning when a commotion commenced amongst the firmly cemented stones set the previous day. Stone after stone, and they were very large ones if one can judge from those used in the construction of the present house, rose in the air of its own accord and then toppled over. Nothing wraith-like or ghostly was seen until the whole structure was demolished. A voice, however, was distinctly heard to utter these words:

> Callaly Castle stands on a height;
> It's up in the day and down at night;
> Set it up on the Shepherd's Shaw,
> There it will stand and never fa';

There is a footnote to this account of Callaly's "ghost" in *The Monthly Chronicle* of 1889 to the effect that the more prosaic explanation of this delightful legend is that Callaly's lady took a dislike to the exposed, inaccessible, crag site and so she had a servant imitate a wild boar who would rootle out the stones as they were placed in position. It is a nice story, anyway.

From the road which runs from Rothbury to Alnwick can be seen some of the best views in the county of Northumberland. An increasing number of cars park along the verges of the highway every day and particularly over the week-ends so that their inmates can enjoy the scenery. In the valley, between the New Moor cross-roads and the high ground by Hulne Park, is the ruined castle of Edlingham. As it is close to the old many-arched railway viaduct it is easily overlooked. It may, however, be found on any large-scale map of the county. The Witch of Edlingham, as has already been stated, was a considerable character. Her name was Margaret Stothard and for a time she was believed to have taken up her residence in the old castle. She was possibly a medium, had clairvoyant powers and she may well have been some sort of a hypnotist. Most witches, to some extent, had such powers. Stothard may well have had gypsy blood in her. A witch in the old days was nearly always associated with the Devil, his handmaid in fact. Female sorcerers would appear to have outnumbered males because it was believed that women, being the weaker vessels, could the more easily be prevailed upon by the Devil.

In England the witch-hunt mania was at its zenith during the sixteenth and seventeenth centuries. By Statute thirty-three of Henry VIII the law adjudged all witchcraft to be felony and so the perpetrators were liable to the death sentence.

In the City of Newcastle upon Tyne one warlock and fourteen witches were tried and convicted at the Assizes in 1649-50 and they were all executed. 3,000 persons, conceived to be guilty of witchcraft, were legally condemned to death during the Commonwealth era.

The depositions against Margaret Stothard, when she was eventually apprehended, tell their own story. These are given in detail in Mackenzie's *History of Northumberland*. They were taken on the 22nd of January 1683 before Mr. Henry Ogle, J.P. One John Mills was the first witness. He said that whilst he was trying to get to sleep a great blast of wind struck the house. Something fell on his body which gave a cry like a catte, then a light appeared at the foot of his bed with the vision of Margaret in it. From the evidence given it would seem that John Mills was scarcely "of sound mind". On occasions his family were known to have had to use force to restrain him - an epileptic perhaps?

The second to appear against Stothard was one William Collingwood of Edlingham. He deposed that eight or nine years previously Jane Carr of Lemendon had spoken of Margaret Stothard as a healer and had then taken her ailing child to her for a cure. Such cure Margaret provided, in physical form, by putting her mouth against that of the child when she made chirping and sucking noises as if she had drawn the child's heart out. After this performance Margaret handed the child back to its parents. This incident is interesting as in its description it sounds exactly like the now modern and generally accepted practice of oral resuscitation.

Jacob Mills of Edlingham Castle told a somewhat similar but less likely story of Margaret Stothard being called to a sick child, the offspring of Alexander Nicholl of Lorbottle, who eventually died. Margaret, as she left this case was said to have fluttered a white kerchief which was taken to be a form of curse.

The final witness was one Isabel Maine of Shawdon. Isabel, a spinster, stated that her cow's milk had gone sour; she had called in the witch. Margaret Stothard had given her salt and herbs to cure the acidity. There is no record as to whether this cure worked. The evidence of the spinster Maine appears to have been taken merely as additional material to try and prove Margaret's wizardry. Strangely there is nothing to suggest that Margaret Stothard, the so-called Witch of Edlingham, was arraigned, nor is there any evidence to suggest that she did not eventually die in her bed or in a ditch. Neither does she appear to have been hunted to death as was the fate, in those days, of so many so-called witches. Maybe Margaret's cures and good works far exceeded her few curses and premonitions of evils to come.

THE VAMPIRE OF BERWICK
and
THE BURNING MAN OF EBCHESTER

Fire is the link in these two strange cases of the occult. Fire in the form of cremation in the former and a curious instance of self-combustion in the latter. From Berwick on Tweed to Ebchester is a long drive in a car today. Should you know the shortest route it will take you all of two to three hours with your foot fairly well down on the accelerator pedal. The distance covers very nearly the whole length of the long, drawn-out county of Northumberland. Ebchester is on the Newcastle-Shotley Bridge road in the Derwent valley. Berwick, as most men know, stands at the mouth of the Tweed which provides, for a part of its length, the Anglo-Scottish Border.

Why the Berwick phantom was named a Vampire it is not easy to explain because this discarnate spirit does not appear to have gone in for any blood-sucking and my dictionary specifically states that a vampire is a form of blood-sucking ghost. The so-called Vampire of Berwick was said to be the nightly spectre of a wealthy citizen of the town which was always closely pursued by a pack of howling hounds. This man of Berwick during his life had evidently done some dissolute deeds. He appears to have been a bit of a rascal if not an out and out rogue. The tale of this haunting has been told by one William, Canon of Newburg Priory in the East Riding of Yorkshire. William has been described as one of the most, veracious and highly esteemed of English Church historians. Unfortunately no names are mentioned as to who the Vampire was, nor are they given of any of the other personalities involved. The Vampire had died after a brief illness, almost certainly the plague which was then raging in the north. Canon William has described the pestilence in these words "Never did it so furiously rage elsewhere". This, of course, is an exaggeration. That the town of Berwick was a serious sufferer there is no doubt for it has been recorded that "it carried off the greater proportion of its inhabitants". But then in Northumberland, and other parts of Britain as well, whole villages were not infrequently eliminated by the bubonic plague.

After the Vampire's burial in unsanctified ground and the various hauntings the townsfolk of Berwick became much terrified. A series of meetings were held and volunteers were called upon to excavate the body, cut it up and burn it. The main fear, apart from the supernatural, was that the ghost of a man dead of the plague could spread it further. Canon William does not say whether the drastic treatment meted out to the corpse of the Vampire exorcised its phantom but one can only assume so. The Canon appears to have been a sincere spiritualist as in his various writings he has instanced a number of other dead men whose discarnate bodies floated around the countryside. Names, as usual, are not given.

The Burning Man of Ebchester is an altogether different story. For here we have plenty of names including such famous ones as that of the Reverend John Wesley, forthright speaker and founder of the Wesleyan Church. Wesley was evidently so impressed with the account of the Burning Man that he is said to have recorded the case in his "Journals" as an instance of unexplained supernatural phenomena. Eric Foster in his version of The Burning Man, which he has included in his *Weird Tales of Northumbria*, writes that Wesley visited the North East on at least thirty-six occasions. His acquaintanceship with this strange instance of internal-combustion appears to have taken place on one of them.

In life the Burning Man was one Mr. Robert Johnson, described as "gentleman", a not uncommon description in those days of a man of good social position usually endowed with land or some other personal means. Family troubles seem to have set off the eventual conflagration because when Johnson's son Cuthbert got married without his parents' consent Old Johnson swore "I hope my right arm will burn off before I give my son sixpence".

Later the families were reconciled and presumably Johnson senior went to his death in peace but his corpse was not so quiescent. At the wake a smell of burning was noticed coming from the coffin. It got worse. The room filled with fumes and a nauseating odour of roasting flesh. The casket was hurriedly opened when it was discovered that old Johnson's right arm had been almost completely incinerated!

THE HEDLEY KOW AND THE LARK HALL SPRITE

Here we have two rather more endearing legends of the spiritual world. The Hedley Kow was a ghost of the bovine race. The Lark Hall sprite, on the other hand, was obviously a discarnate human spirit of a rather mischievous character but so was the Kow! That is why I have decided to include these two tales of the supernatural in the same chapter.

The locality frequented by the Kow has not been definitely pinpointed, it might have been any of the Durham Hedleys. For there is a Hedley by Mickley, Ebchester, Whittonstall, Blackburn Pell, Lanchester and Cornsay. Whichever was the chosen site is no great matter for many of these Hedleys are not far distant the one from the other. Apart from the Hedleys one place the Kow appears to have favoured was Hamsterley Hall, the house once occupied by Robert Smith Surtees who could tell a ghost story with the best, and now the residence of Lord Gort.

The Kow, unlike so many other ghosts, does not appear to have associated much with death for she seems to have preferred a house of birth rather than the place where man's soul had recently parted from his body. This mischievous sprite would possess the horse on whose pillion the midwife rode, making the animal play-up whilst fording a stream. Also in her own guise as a cow she would bellow through the window during an accouchement and when chased away would lure her pursuers into mires.

Although mainly an animal ghost the Kow, on occasion, could assume unusual forms such as ambulent hayricks and pretty girls who would lure lonely country bumpkins into all sorts of unenvious situations. This spook certainly appears to have been capricious rather than terrifying. *The Monthly Chronicle* of 1889 gives some good examples of the Kow's mischievous doings. There is the account of the farmer by the name of Forster who lived at one of the Hedleys. At dawn one day this man went out to harness his old grey mare to the trap for a shopping trip to Newcastle. Half way down the lane the cob slipped its traces and then with a snicker proceeded to kick the upturned vehicle into pieces - it was the Hedley Kow.

The Kow, as one might expect, was fond of teasing dairy-maids and frequenting milking parlours where she would upset pails, kick over stools and even imitate the low moaning voices of the dairy-maids' love-lorn suitors. The Kow's favourite trick was to possess a placid milk-cow, refuse to give milk, slip its collar, knock over anything in sight and then take to the fields frantically pursued by some rosy-cheeked buxom belle of the bucket.

Perhaps the most amusing tale of the Kow's adventures is that told by Stephen Oliver in his *Rumbles in Northumberland*, for here it is related that two lonely men were on their way home in the gloaming, both scared and fearful of meeting the Kow. When one heard the other behind him he commenced to canter and then gallop. His pursuer hearing the hoof-beats joined in the race, also believing the Kow was after him. When finally the leader was overhauled, exhausted and sweating, his pursuer was heard to inquire:

"In the name of the Father and of the Son and the Holy Ghost, who art thou?"

The answer came in a quavering voice.

"A-a's Johnie Brown o' the High Fields. Who's thoo?"

In January 1800 a mischievous spirit invaded the premises of Lark Hall near Burrowdon, in the parish of Alwinton in the upper Coquet valley. The site of Lark Hall is marked on most ordnance maps.

Lark Hall was a small farm house which belonged to a Mr. William Walby of Burrowdon who rented it to a Mr. Turnbull, butcher of Rothbury. The Turnbulls shared the dwelling with an old hind and his family, there being only a partition between the two families. The Sprite appeared to have strong poltergeistic powers - at first it was suspected that the house was haunted for noises and knockings were heard in various parts of the house. The plates, bowls, basins, glasses and tea cups used to jump off the shelves and break. The chairs and tables danced about the rooms in a most fantastic manner. Such phenomena in other places are still being recorded. In the first chapter of this book the case of the "haunted" house at Lanchester, Co. Durham, is mentioned where in 1971 bumps, thumps, and similar disturbances could not be accounted for.

One of the Sprite's more curious tricks was played in the presence of the Reverend Lauder, minister at Harbottle, who came to administer some solace and consolation to the affected inmates. The reverend gentleman had scarcely arrived when the large Holy Book, which was lying on the window recess, made a sudden series of gyrations through the air to fall at the clergyman's feet. All these incidents were verified by creditable witnesses. Two professional magicians were brought in besides intelligent investigators who carefully examined the premises but failed utterly to discover anything which could account for these strange happenings.

Eventually a reward of twenty pounds (an appreciable sum in 1800) was offered to anyone able to solve this mystery but the money was never claimed, nor was the Sprite or its doings ever clearly explained. I think one might be permitted to wonder whether one of the Turnbulls, or a member of the hind's family, was a medium, for mediums have been known to do some quite wonderful things.

Great mediums like Daniel Dunglas Home, the Reverend Stainton Moses and Mrs. Lenore Piper have done much more remarkable things than did the Sprite. From all the evidence available, and there is a very great deal, none of the mediums mentioned here were in any sense fakes. Home for one never took money for his services. Men of the calibre of the Earl of Dunraven who was twice Under-Secretary of State for the Colonies, the Earl of Crawford, a Fellow of the Royal Society and President of the Royal Astronomical Society, Sir William Crookes, who was knighted for his services to science and later received the Order of Merit, all believed and were presumably satisfied that these mediums were endowed with remarkable supernatural powers far in excess of any of those possessed by the Sprite.

THE BROWN MAN OF THE MOORS AND THE SIMONSIDE DWARFS

I have spent much time up in the hills and on the moors looking for the Brown Man but unfortunately I have never been successful in encountering him or his kind but I have had other adventures and some of them interesting ones too. The Simonside Hills are a favourite haunt of mine and old ruins like Blackcock Castle are a sheer delight. It was when I was up near the Castle that I came across the young man whom I chose to call The Snake Boy of Chartners, but more of the Snake Boy later and back to legend.

George Taylor in his *A Memoir of Robert Surtees, Esq., M.A., F.S.A.*, quotes a letter from Surtees to Walter Scott in which Surtees discusses "The Brown Man of the Muirs". He tells Scott that the legend, was related to him (Surtees) by one Elizabeth

Cockburn of Offerton.

This may suggest to some of us that the story of "The Brown Man" was one of Surtees' clever fabrications. Many of Robert Surtees' stories have old ladies as narrators. It is possible that Elizabeth Cockburn was a fictitious character. Nevertheless "The Brown Man" has now become a part of the folklore of Northumberland and bears repeating.

The scene of the story is the moorland about Elsdon which is adjacent to and contiguous with the Simonside range of hills. Two young men from the city of Newcastle decided to have a day's sporting on the hills about Elsdon. They were probably out on a quiet poaching expedition. Tired, they sat down in a quiet green glade and had a drink from the clear water of the little burn which flowed through it. When they had both quenched their thirst they looked up to see a little brown human-being about half the size of a normal man. He is described as being stout and broad having an appearance of immense strength. He was dressed entirely in brown homespun the colour of dead bracken. His head was covered in frizzled red hair. His facial expression is said to have been ferocious whilst his eyes resembled those of an enraged bull. He sounds to have been a very angry little man.

The dwarf inquired of one of the young men if he knew who he was, when the lad tactfully replied that he assumed him to be The Lord of the Manor. The youngster also added that he was quite willing to hand over the game that he had got. This offer appears to have placated the little brown man who refused the proffered game and said he himself was a vegetarian living on whortle-berries, cloud-berries, dew-berries and crane-berries with nuts and mushrooms for a change. In winter, the dwarf went on, my food is hazelnuts and crab apples, wild plums and sloes, of which I have a great store in the woods. The brown man then invited the young sportsmen to come and partake of his hospitality. The younger of the two turned to his elder companion to get his agreement but when he looked around to accept the dwarf's invitation the little brown man had completely disappeared. The sequel to this tale writes Surtees, as told to him by Elizabeth

Cockburn, was that the younger of the two youths, he who appears to have done most of the talking with the dwarf, caught a lingering chill on his return to Newcastle to die before the year was out. People, of course, were inclined to blame the Little Brown Man for the youngster's unfortunate demise and not the probable fact that he had caught his death of a cold.

The story of the Simonside Dwarfs, told in *The Monthly Chronicle* of 1891, has a certain similarity, only few names are given of persons or places. The little men are of demoniac appearance, clad in dark-green and brown. These elves are small in size, even smaller than the Brown Man of the Moors. They were said to carry lights at night so as to lead unwary travellers to their domains amongst the bogs and mires. Shepherds, out at all hours of the day and night, were their main witnesses. One sophisticated soul who, even in the time of the dwarfs, would not have anything to do with such beliefs as kelpies, ghosts, brownies and mystical dwarfs, announced publicly that such elves as those of Simonside were probably wild animals or night birds. He maintained that the dwarfs were a pure myth and that the noises, shrieks and howls were those of buzzards, shrikes, drumming snipe, booming bitterns and honking wild geese. He told how on one occasion he himself had heard Roarie, as the leader of the Dwarfs was known. Roarie proved to have been a tawny owl. To prove his disbelief in the supernatural this sceptic of old, decided to spend a night out on the wilds of Simonside. With a warm plaid and a stout staff he set out on his all-night journey. Suddenly, in the pitch darkness when the gloaming had gone he saw, in the distance, a number of small lights. These waned and flickered and were quite inexplicable. He was frightened. He decided to make for home, when he felt he was being followed. Three brawny, tiny demons appeared bearing lighted faggots to bar his way. Others of similar appearance came on the scene. The sceptic was surrounded. In mad panic he battered his way, with the aid of his stout staff, through the ring of demons. He fainted. Dawn revived him. He returned fortunately none the worse but a less boastful man.

As I have already stated I have never been so fortunate as

to have met the Little People but on one occasion when I was out walking one evening near Blackcock Castle I did meet a most unusual character. The boy was small and auburn-haired, dressed in a dark green anorak and tight blue jeans. His hair, as is now the fashion, was long, reaching well down the nape of his neck. He carried an air rifle in the crotch of his right arm. From his left hand something dangled like a short length of rope. On closer examination I saw the rope was an adder. He looked, for all the world, like some sort of modern Daniel Boone.

"What have you got there?" I asked him.

"Viper" he said "I loathe them".

Under the title of "The Snake Boy of Chartners" I wrote this story up in some detail when it was eventually published in one of our national weekly magazines. There are plenty of adders still up on the Simonside hills but so far as I know no dwarfs or little brown men.

THE KNARESDALE HALL GHOST
and
THE HEADLESS GHOST OF WATTON ABBEY

Knaresdale Hall, once the property of the Pratt family, is situated about four miles south of Haltwhistle in splendid "ghost" country. Once again our friend William Pattison, but this time of Tow Law and not of Bishopwearmouth, as in previous recordings, relates the story of the Knaresdale Ghost in Richardson's *Local Historian's Table Book*. William Pattison, of course, may well have resided at different times at both Tow Law and Bishopwearmouth. Unfortunately I have not been able, in my researches, to find out very much about William Pattison. He seems to have been an interesting local character who specialised in tales and legends of the occult. His name crops up time and time again in the five large volumes of *The Monthly Chronicle* (1887-1891). Richardson also quotes him frequently in his Table Book.

The story of the Knaresdale Ghost is a gruesome one and it

involves the very rare crime of a brother killing his sister. One of the main characters in this story is the Laird, or lord of the manor of Knaresdale. He was a man of middle age when he married. He is described as being selfish, irritable and well-sunk in the ways of bachelor-hood. Against her will he married a pretty girl of good family, with her parents' consent. This young lady appears to have had a will of her own. Perhaps quite naturally the marriage did not flourish; more exactly it could be described as a matrimonial disaster. Matters became more complicated in Knaresdale Hall when the Laird somewhat quixotically undertook to house and care for a niece and nephew of his who had been recently orphaned. The boy was about eighteen whilst his sister was a year younger. It was perhaps quite to be expected that trouble started almost at once. The boy fell for the young wife who seems to have been far from reluctant to receive his advances. The possibility is that the old Laird was impotent, if not a rather ineffective lover. The illicit affair went on apace until one evening the young man's sister caught the mistress of the house and her brother in an embrace. She was horrified at what she saw. The cat was out of the bag with a vengeance. Her brother and his mistress were fearful that she might expose them. The murder was then plotted.

On a bitter-cold, wild night of wind and rain, the young wife aroused her husband from a deep slumber to complain that she could not sleep because of a door banging outside. She urged the Laird to send his niece out to shut it. Reluctantly, for the sake of his rest, if nothing else, he called to his niece to get up and shut the door. The girl complied with his request and when she got outside her brother caught her and plunged her into a deep pond where she was drowned. Not hearing his niece come back into the house the old Laird became worried and told his wife to get up and see if she was back in bed. The Laird's wife appears to have been able to placate him by telling him that the girl was probably safely sleeping, having crept in quietly so as not to disturb them. The Laird dozed off, suddenly to be wakened by the howl of what sounded like a dog, and then at the foot of his bed the phantom appeared of a young girl, her hair dripping wet and dishevelled. The old man tried to speak to the apparition but his voice failed him.

Next day with the disappearance of the Laird's niece her brother was also missing. The wife at first attributed their joint departure to their unhappiness or discontent. Her conscience however then began to trouble her for she was certainly a party to the murder. She went raving mad and eventually in her babblings she exposed the plot and the subsequent murder. The pond was dragged and the body and remains of a young female were brought to light. The murderer appears never to have been apprehended, During wild windy nights on the anniversary of this cold-blooded murder doors bang and the apparition of a wet, distraught young girl walks the corridors of Knaresdale.

The Headless Ghost of Watton Abbey seems to be a rather nebulous spectre. The phantom is supposed to be that of a murdered woman and her child. Some years ago a visitor to Watton, who knew nothing of this apparition, slept in the wainscoted room, when in the night he was visited by the ghost of a lady whose garments appeared to be soaked in blood. The lady's murder has been attributed to the licentious soldiery but details are notable for their absence. There is no authenticated history of this headless phantom, merely a persistent but urgent legend which has been handed down with the rather unusual story of Watton Abbey itself. The Abbey, or what remains of it, is situated between Beverley and Driffield. This foundation was said to have been laid down by one Eustace Fitz-John in expiation of his loose life and as a penance for his crimes. Prior to this the monastery was believed to have been destroyed by the Danes at the same time as the bigger ecclesiastical establishment at Beverley was demolished. The Scandinavian vandals may have been responsible for the headless woman or possibly it may have been a later monastic murder committed during Henry VIII's reign when so many religious establishments suffered from fire, sword and the axe under the orders of Thomas Cromwell, known as "The Hammer of the Monks".

The influence of Eustace Fitz-John's habits in life appear to have somehow percolated down through the centuries in the manner of living of the succeeding inhabitants of the Abbey.

At one time both nuns and monks cohabited in this establishment and they appear to have had a profligate time together in the tradition of their founder. In 1326 William de Melton, Archbishop of York consecrated no less than fifty-three nuns at one session. The words "rather loose" appear in the history of Watton Abbey as recorded in *The Monthly Chronicle* of 1888.

The ghost of Watton was certainly not laid in the eighteenth century for there is an interesting and somewhat amusing account of Watton's haunting which took place in 1788. This was when the Bethell family was in possession of the Abbey. The rector of Lockinton, a small parish near Watton, was dining one evening with the Bethells when strange thumps and noises started to emanate from beneath the dining room table. These "manifestations" continued on subsequent occasions. Eventually, unable to endure the thumps and bumps any longer the Bethells had the floor of the dining room taken up, when a bitch otter and her litter were found to have taken up their residence in the foundations!

THE CAULD LAD OF HYLTON

No-one could say today that Hylton is a place of any great beauty. It is, in fact, one of the less attractive parts of our two northern counties. Situated between Monkwearmouth and Gateshead, in the north of Co. Durham, it is largely an industrialised area. In all fairness to Hylton however it should be said that the announcer on the eight o' clock B.B.C. news on January 28th 1971, stated that certain local enthusiasts had plans in hand to improve some of Hylton's amenities. Details as to what such amenities were, or how they were likely to be improved, were not elaborated upon.

Hylton Castle, which is the site favoured by the ghost of the Cauld Lad is a peculiar structure and considering its great age it is in a remarkable state of preservation. The Cauld Lad has been described as a bar-guest or local sprite. Sprite my dictionary informs me is a mischievous spirit, fairy or elf. Fairies need no explanation, being pretty, attractive beings of much charm. There are also gnomes and goblins, variously described as earth spirits living underground and mischievous, ugly demons. Oliver Hyslop's admirable book *Northumberland Words* says that bar-guest means a boggle and he suggests the word is derived from the German *berg-geist*, a mountain demon or gnome.

Bar-guest, or sprite, the Cauld Lad is certainly no ghoul or ghastly phantom but rather a delightful little being who occasionally bursts out into attractive verse - some of it one cannot help thinking having been composed by that puckish author, historian and antiquarian Robert Surtees of Mainsforth. But more of R.S., in this connection, later.

The Hyltons of Hylton had a fabulous genealogy extending back to the times of Athelstan (895) and a genuine pedigree which commenced with the reign of Henry II (1133). The origin of the family is unknown. Hyltons had served in the Crusades, were present at the Battle of Lewes (1264), and one member of the family is known to have joined in the famed Pilgrimage of Grace in 1536. The castle is said to have been built between 1435-1447. The last Hylton died in 1746 and the properties, amounting to several thousand acres surrounding the castle, were sold by auction in 1750.

The Cauld Lad which is a comparatively recent addition to the family only came into existence circa 1600 about a century and a half before the last of the Hyltons went over himself into the spirit world. Robert Surtees has recorded the fact that he received information concerning this bar-guest or local sprite from one J. B. Taylor, Esquire. Surtees has gone away here from his usual sources of legends and folklore as so many of these creations of his were supplied to him by some old dame or crone. The Cauld Lad's ghost is said to be that of a young stable boy who was accidentally killed by a Hylton with a scythe. There are other versions; namely that in irritation at finding the boy asleep in a hay loft, and his horse unsaddled, the said Hylton tried to rouse him with a hay fork and stabbed the lad to death. Fearful of the consequences the laird dumped the corpse in a pond where some years later the body was discovered. The pith of these tales may lie in the records of the coroner's inquest of July 3rd 1609 on the body of a youth, one Roger Skelton, who was killed with the point of a scythe accidentally applied by one Robert Hylton of Hylton. Hylton received a free pardon on the 6th September 1609. Why the Cauld Lad's spirit is not more sinister it is hard to understand for the boy certainly met a horrible death if it were by misadventure or murder.

It was from this incident presumably that the poem entitled "The Cauld Lad O' Hylton" came to be written. May one be allowed to assume by Surtees? The fact that the title has been apostrophised makes one a trifle suspicious. The ballad does not confine the sprite's activities to the castle of Hylton and like the kelpies of Scotland "The Cauld Lad" was said to row people over the Wear in a ferry-boat stationed near the grounds of the castle. He never drowned his human cargo, however, as the kelpie is said to do, but used to abandon his passengers in mid-Wear by vanishing into thin air!

About the house, the Lad was an adroit poltergeist upsetting furniture, chattels, the silver and so on. Should the maids tidy up, the Cauld Lad would disarray, should the domestics leave things awry he would put things in order. At one time the Lad's attentions became so persistent that an attempt was made to have the ghost exorcised by the customary procedure of calling in the priest. One thing appears to be certain: any such laying of this uncivil spirit was conducted long after the last of the Hyltons went the way of all flesh, as the voice of the Cauld Lad was heard, on various occasions, two centuries after the end of the line.   There is one particularly attractive story about the Lad, when he was presumably at his most active and mischievous stage. The laundry was in a turmoil, the kitchen in an upheaval and the dining-room in a mess. The maids were frantic. The Lad must be dissuaded from his levitations and disturbances. A tiny cape and cloak in hunter's green were made for the use of this mischievous sprite. Laid out on the sideboard it was a tempting bait and accepted, but the Cauld Lad presumably made it quite clear that this conciliatory attempt at exorcism was not likely to be effective, because in the dead of night after the cloak and cape had disappeared a disembodied voice was heard to chant:

> "Wae's me, wae's me
> The acorn is not yet
> Fallen from the tree
> That's to grow the wood
> That's to make the cradle
> That's to rock the bairn
> That's to grow a man
> That's to lay me"

Do we hear the flavour of Robert Surtees' rhyme and rhythm?

I spent a very pleasant morning in March this year inspecting Hylton Castle with John Green the Custodian. Hylton Castle is now in the keeping of the Department of Environment. Mr. Green's trouble was not ghosts, but vandals. Only the previous night some oafs had tried to dig into the vaults. Previously a massive oak door had been smashed and wrenched off its hinges. Hylton and its purlieus today would appear to be vandal terrain rather than ghost-country.

THE WILLINGTON GHOST

The Willington ghost is possibly one of the most publicised spiritual manifestations in Northumberland. The story, in its day, received a considerable press mainly because of the subsequent attempts which were made to probe the mystery. It is a comparatively recent ghost story the actual house in which the events occurred having been built in 1806. The period of the hauntings took place between 1840-1845.

Willington lies between North Shields and Wallsend, almost due north across the Tyne from Hylton. It now consists of even less salubrious surroundings than Hylton's. At the time of the alleged poltergeistic occurrences at Hylton, and subsequently those at Willington, these two now densely populated areas would not have been so populous as they are now; they were nonetheless far from deserted. Willington Mill was a busy place in an already industrialised area in the nineteenth century. Somehow, one does not expect ghosts in built-up areas, yet they occur. The case at Lanchester in Co. Durham, already mentioned and which only happened a few weeks ago, is a recent case. The Lanchester poltergeistic occurrences were investigated by priest, press, radio, television, not to mention the Society for Psychical Research and all parties, to some degree or another, appeared to have sensed or felt something.

The story of the Willington ghost is rather vague. The apparition responsible for the sounds and movements occasionally reported is supposed to have been that of a person foully murdered. No names, no dates or any other useful evidence are available. The phenomena observed or heard are described as thuds, staircase rattlings, patter of bare
feet, closets opening and rarely the appearance in shadowy form of an old man and a woman both with heads depressed and the woman eyeless.

Willington Mill was at the time of the visitations a substantial flour mill, the property of Messrs. Unthank & Procter. Joseph Procter lived in the Mill House when in 1840 the manifestations became more pronounced. Because of the activity and prolonged period during which the unaccounted for noises in the night continued it was decided to investigate the site of these occurrences to try and ascertain whether any mundane explanation could be found. The Procter family, themselves then living at the Mill House, do not appear to have been unduly disturbed by the atmosphere of their residence. They seem to have taken the bumps and thumps with unusual phlegm.

Through the personal friendship of the Procters with a Dr. Edward Drury an investigation was commenced. The Doctor, who was obviously deeply interested in the cause of these spiritualistic manifestations, was able to recruit the assistance of a local chemist in North Shields, one Thomas Hudson. Together these two men went through the customary investigations. Drury, for safety's sake, armed himself with a brace of loaded pistols but these appear to have been forgotten for they were certainly not brought into action. Candles were used and the two men sat up until past midnight when something started to happen. Later Dr. Drury wrote down his experience. The following is a brief extract.

"... I took up a note which I had accidentally dropped and began to read it; after which I took out my watch to ascertain the time. In taking my eyes from the watch they became riveted upon a closet door which I distinctly saw open, and also saw the figure of a female attired in greyish garments, with the head inclined downwards, and one hand pressed upon the chest as if in pain, and the other - the right hand - extended towards the floor, with the index finger pointing downwards. It advanced with an apparently cautious step across the floor towards me. Immediately as it approached my friend (the chemist Hudson) who was dozing, its right hand extended towards him. I then rushed at it, giving at the same time a most awful yell but, instead of grasping it, I fell upon my friend. I recollected nothing distinctly for nearly three hours afterwards. I have since learnt that I was carried downstairs in an agony of fear and terror".

This sounds a most factual account of what Dr. Drury obviously thought he had seen. One immediately suspects a nightmare but the experiences of others such as two young ladies whose bed was levitated violently on one occasion and the frequent appearance of shadowy figures in the windows of the house, the repeated footsteps, curtain drawings and other ghostly appearances would all seem to permit one to dismiss the nightmare theory.

Later the chemist Hudson set down on paper his own account of the night spent in Willington Mill House with his friend Dr. Drury. He writes:

"His (Dr. Drury's) hair was standing on end, the picture of

horror. He fainted, and fell into my arms, like a lifeless piece of humanity. His horrible shouts had made me shout in sympathy and I instantly laid him down and went into the room from whence the last sound was heard. But nothing was there and the window had not been opened. Mr. Procter and the housekeeper came quickly to our assistance, and found the young doctor trembling in acute mental agony. Indeed, he was so much excited that he wanted to jump out of the window".

Hudson obviously had suffered from no nightmares although after being wakened from his dozing he had evidently heard something, apart from Drury's ravings, for he went to the room next door from which he thought he heard queer noises.

These written records are of particular interest because, I think, they personify the characters of the two individuals. Edward Drury highly strung but brave, for he not only was prepared to face the ghost but was also courageous enough to admit and write down his abject terror. Thomas Hudson more phlegmatic but quite prepared to follow up the phantom. Later a Mr. Howitt, author of *Visits to Remarkable Places* (1840-1841) also investigated this ghost but he has added little to what was already known and has been reported here.

THE LUMLEY GHOST STORY

This is no story of ancient castles or great haunted mansions; it is rather the interesting record of how the ghost of a murdered person came to a man, who was, perhaps, an unconscious medium, to name and to accuse her murderers. Once again Surtees has related the circumstances and this time they sound most convincing. Time and time again through history we have similar cases - the warning or advice from the other side of places where violence has been committed and of the persons involved. The curious manner in which some murders of the past and, for that matter, of the present have been revealed in dreams is no new thing.

The age-old saying "That murder will out" has been substantiated more than once by some waking vision or some nightmare experience.

The Lumley Ghost Story has also been called The Chester le Street Murder and I have no doubt has been related under various other titles. The essentials, however, in all these recordings, are the same. The one which appears in Robert Surtees' *History of Durham* is as good as any and this is surely the prototype from which the many other versions have been compiled.

This story of murder in a small village in Durham travelled far and wide in the seventeenth century, eventually reaching as far as London. Briefly, one John Walker, a yeoman of good estate and a widower, had living with him in his house in Chester le Street a comely young female relative called Anne Walker. Anne presumably looked after him. That he had an affair with her, or possibly seduced her, seems almost certain. Anxious to get rid of her when she became pregnant John Walker got as his accomplice a pitman by the name of Mark Sharp. Sharp appears to have been a brutal type, as Walker surely knew he was. Sharp was the hatchet man, Walker the instigator of the crime. Suddenly, Anne Walker disappeared from her Chester le Street home. John Walker said she had gone back to her relatives. Now we have the go-between, or certainly psychic, to whom the crime came as a vision. John Grahame was not at all a superstitious man until this occasion. In the early part of the seventeenth century it would have been a brave man to openly laugh at ghosts, spectres, goblins, sprites and other allied demonstrations of the supernatural. Grahame would have none of these things in spite of the fact that he was eventually proved to have strong telepathic powers.

Grahame would work all hours as long as the corn came in from the farmers to be ground. One evening he was working away filling sacks when a woman appeared smothered in blood. She had the most ghastly head wounds, five in number, and her blonde hair was soaked in gore. Staunch man though he was Grahame was deeply shocked but he appears to have been able to question the phantom girl to ask her purpose. "I am the spirit of Anne Walker murdered by the collier Mark Sharp. He has buried the pick, his blood soaked shoes and stockings under a bank, Now it is up to you to reveal the truth".

The miller was in a quandary; he knew nothing of the Chester le Street murder; had he seen a vision; had he been dreaming; was this just a hallucination? All these thoughts passed through his mind. He decided to say nothing. He quietened his internal tensions in the belief that he had been out of sorts that evening. Nevertheless, he did cease to work alone late at nights in the mill. Grahame's wife appears to have been pleased to be able to see more of her husband. The ghost of Anne Walker, however, was a most persistent one. It was not going to allow Grahame, her sole communication with the living, to rest. On two subsequent occasions the dead Anne Walker, in all her gruesome gore, accosted the miller. She revealed not only where the instrument of her death lay but where her own body was to be found in a coal shaft close by. By the time she came to Grahame for the third time she seems to have become almost violently insistent that her murder be reported.

Finally Grahame went to the magistrates who rather surprisingly, I think, accepted the miller's very unusual story. Subsequent investigations revealed the pick, boots, stockings and corpse exactly where the ghost had said they were. John Walker and Mark Sharp were apprehended. They were both found guilty of the murder of Anne Walker before Judge Davenport in August 1631. Condemned to death, they were duly executed. This remarkable revelation and subsequent discovery of a cruel murder quite naturally caused a considerable sensation at the time.

Such remarkable telepathic or spiritual manifestations as this one have happened since. Even now the police are sometimes approached by completely sincere individuals who claim to have had communications from those recently deceased and particularly, perhaps, from those unfortunates who have sneered a sudden or shocking death. Many spiritualists believe that a murdered man's or woman's spirit is more reluctant to leave the mundane body than that of one who dies a peaceful death. Lord Dowding has claimed, with utter sincerity and obvious belief, that he has communicated on many occasions through mediums with the R.A.F. pilots who died in a violent manner during the Battle of Britain. The soul or spirit of such brave men, Dowding says, clings to the earth and only gradually ascends to other astral spheres.

Battlefields are believed to have an aura of haunting about them. Many men claim to have seen the apparition of armed men and armies in the vicinity of these once blood-stained places. My friend Jim Wentworth Day, journalist and author - he has written two books on ghosts and has done a considerable amount of research concerning the occult - swears he saw a ghostly horde over the Somme battlefields in the winter of 1918. J.W.D. was then an officer in charge of a small German P.O.W. camp. He had gone out with his batman to commandeer some rations. In the light of the setting sun he saw, suddenly, on the horizon a squadron of German Uhlans with their odd-shaped, flat-topped helmets and coming towards them a squadron of French Dragoons mounted on their stout, close-coupled, weight-carrying chargers. The war was over. Cavalry in 1918 had virtually had it. Yet the locality, where Day saw this ghostly horde, was once fought over by such mounted units. Jim has made the point in relating this episode that he does not believe in ghosts nor is he psychic, although he is prepared to swear on his life that what he witnessed that evening was true. I believe him. Then there is the now world-famed "Angel of Mons" - a fantastic vision seen by hundreds of different people. There is no need to repeat this legend as it is so well known.

Unfortunately murders today are almost daily events. One only has to pick up any paper and one is sure to read therein of some act of violence and death. The murders of the present time are just as vicious and gruesome as that of Anne Walker. The recent case of the woman at Standagainstall farm in County Durham is a case in point. The husband, with the aid of two accomplices, brutally killed his wife and buried her body nearby. The motive of this crime appears to have been quite senseless. Children are killed almost daily. It is frightening. One can only wish that there were more Grahames about to whom the guilty parties of so many of these modern murders could be immediately revealed.</p>

THE LONG PACK

The Long Pack is the story of the attempted robbery of a rich gentleman's country house in the valley of the North Tyne; how the burglars gained entry and the effective defence put up by a single domestic female and two farm workers. Described like this the tale may not sound much but if you have read it, as you should, and as I have, on numberless occasions, in its original form, it stands out as a gem of the early nineteenth century. This is undoubtedly due to the fact that the account was written by James Hogg, friend of Sir Walter Scott and Robert Surtees. Hogg, at the time he wrote The Long Pack, was said to be a protege of Mr. Scott who was then sheriff of Selkirkshire.

Hogg was known widely as The Ettrick Shepherd under which nom de plume he wrote many poems, ballads and verses. He must have been an extraordinarily versatile man for he could turn out a ballad, a poem, a song or a story with equal ease. Hogg, amongst his many publications, wrote a treatise which he entitled Hogg on Sheep. Amongst James Hogg's many great talents were his abilities to describe his characters so that they come vividly to life. He was also able to paint with his pen the scenes where the events he wrote about took place. Hogg's description of Alice the maid left in charge of the household and one of the main characters in this drama is simply superb; the same applies to Edward the gawky, gun-toting hind who is largely responsible, though entirely fortuitously, in the thwarting of the robber's plan. James Hogg, the Ettrick Shepherd, is acclaimed by many Scotophiles as being as great, if not a greater poet than their beloved Robert Burns. It is of interest to note that Hogg was a regular contributor at one time to *Blackwood's Magazine*, that doyen of monthly periodicals which has helped to launch the works of so many famous authors on to the market.

Few long-short stories have been repeated and reprinted more often than has The Long Pack. Some of these reprints are distorted editions of the original but there are a number which are, in effect, verbatim copies of Hogg's own version. The copy of this story which I obtained at the Newcastle City Library, bound in book form, is surely unadulterated Hogg; so is C. T. Oxley's account in his charming little booklet *Strange Tales and Legends of the North Country*. Frank Graham, the Newcastle publisher, brought out an edition of Hogg's story which was attractively illustrated by Frank Varty of Morpeth. Graham has attributed The Long Pack to Joseph Crawhall. I think this must have come about because the publisher had the tale from a book printed in 1883 entitled "Olde Tayles Newlye Relayted" which was edited by Joseph Crawhall. The Long Pack is the work of James Hogg and no one else. No bowdlerised account can possibly compare with the original - read it, it is easily obtained.

The Long Pack is not a tale of the occult but nevertheless it is an eerie and spine-chilling as the best of ghostlies. Perhaps, not unnaturally, because the actual name of the mansion is not given, the incidents told of have been suggested as having happened at big houses as far apart as Chipchase, La Lee Hall and Swinburne. Both Chipchase and La Lee are at present inhabited. Swinburne lost its roof some years ago and is now derelict. All three of these charming properties can be said to be within the confines of the broad North Tyne valley. Hogg pinpointed the site of his story as having happened in Northumberland and he has added authenticity to his account by naming the owner of the house where the events took place as a Colonel Ridley, a name which is very closely associated with the county. This I feel, gives some idea of how meticulous Hogg could be in giving his accounts strong local colour. That the Long Pack is colourful there is no shadow of doubt.

My own preferred site of this event is La Lee Hall. I fell in love with the place the first time I saw it. La Lee lies on the west bank of the river. It is a square built old white-harled house in pleasant surroundings. At the time I first came upon the house it was untenanted and the garden overgrown but somehow, near derelict as it was then, it had enormous appeal for me. In reading The Long Pack I always see the events that took place on that bitter cold winter night as happening at this small country gentleman's residence rather than at the much more grand castles of Swinburne or Chipchase.

LEE HALL of 'Long Pack' fame

Colonel Ridley, owner of the house, had made a great deal of money in the far east and with this he had bought his place in the country. He also owned a fine collection of silver and valuables all of which he was supposed to have kept in the house. This wealth was the burglar's objective. Ridley, like so many other Northumbrian landed proprietors in those days used to go up to London with his family for a period during the winter to enjoy its high-life and to avoid the cold bleak climate of the north. The burglary therefore had been planned to take place when the family was away. The skeleton staff in the house then consisted of Richard, an old man who threshed the corn, Alice, the housemaid, a most attractive girl, and Edward a young man who helped Richard, herded the cattle and scared the rooks off the corn with the aid of an ancient and much loved muzzle loader which he insisted on calling Copenhagen. Here again we see one of Hogg's masterly little touches. What a magnificent name for a trusty old weapon – Copenhagen!

To those of us who have had much experience of guns and rifles nearly all of these pieces of wood and metal assume in time characters of their very own. They become personalities almost imbued with near-human qualities. This may sound strange to anyone who has no experience of owning sporting firearms but it is very true. A gun or a rifle can be a personality, and old Copenhagen was certainly not only a weapon of immense calibre but also one of great individuality. Edward was no great shot, in fact he appears to have been a poor marksman especially at flying objects as his score of rooks appears to have been pretty meagre. He sometimes blamed his gun for his inaccurate shooting and sometimes himself. Often he wondered whether his charge of powder and shot just evaporated into nothing when birds flew away apparently quite unscathed. The time was shortly to come, however, when fired at a near static object old Copenhagen's blasting capacity was to be most powerfully demonstrated.

On the cold, wet, windy night of this story a pedlar with a great cumbersome pack on his shoulders turns up at the hall to see if he can sell some of his wares. Pedlars, or itinerant merchants, were important persons in those days, as they brought news of events and people from far away. Many who had their regular routes, or rounds, were honest men and well liked but as in the case of all other professions there were rogues amongst the brotherhood. Some pedlars walked, others rode, perhaps, with pack-ponies behind; the occasional traveller of old might have had a horse and cart doing door to door deliveries like the modern Co-op van. The pedlar of the days of The Ettrick Shepherd was the prototype of our present day commercial traveller or sales representative.

The pedlar who arrived at the hall was certainly a plausible, chatty type and after gaining entrance from Alice he quickly made himself at home. He asked if he could stay the night. Alice refused. He made amorous advances. Alice quickly repulsed them. Then in well simulated despair he asked if he could leave his pack in the kitchen whilst he sought shelter elsewhere. Alice gave in. The man disappeared into the darkness outside. In appearance the pack was unusual, being long and not unlike a coffin. Having got rid of her unwelcome guest Alice lit some more candles. Suddenly out of the corner of her eye she thought she saw the pack move. To quote Hogg;

"Every inch of flesh on her body crept like a nest of pismires"

Pismires for the uninitiated are ants!

Alice immediately decided to seek aid. She yelled for old Richard. Old Richard tried to calm the girl's agitation. Whilst the two of them were discussing the pedlar and the queer pack he had left behind, Edward walks in carrying Copenhagen. Edward, in his youthful enthusiasm, is anxious to try out his weapon on the pack. He is temporarily restrained by the other two. But when Edward too thought he saw the pack moving, he fired. There were groans, horrible gutteral sounds and blood gushed out of the big parcel on to the floor. The sounds of anguish ceased. The three servants courageously opened the pack to find a very dead man who had with him in his crate no less than four pistols, a cutlass and what James Hogg describes as "a silver wind-call". It did not take much detective work on the part of the three participants in this drama to realise that the pedlar had planted his accomplice in the hall and that in due time the dead man was to use the wind-call, or whistle, to summon outside aid.

In the crisis Edward, the farm-lad, seems to have assumed considerable stature. He visualises the plot and acts accordingly. Immediately he summons what local help there is nearby. He arms his companions with what weapons are available including the four pistols found in the pack. Having placed his defence forces at strategic windows, Edward blows the wind-call. In the distance the call is answered. Then comes the sound of galloping horses. Mounted men appear in the wan light of the moon. A burst of fire comes from the windows of the hall. Men fall from their horses. Screams and groans rend the air. Copenhagen once again proves its worth as Edward shoots what appears to be the leader almost at the front door. Then the attacking forces are heard to be retreating and a little later the courageous Edward accompanied by another go out to see what damage they have done. They find four dead men scattered about the policies. As it is not yet full light the two return to the hall once more. When dawn duly comes, to the household's amazement, there are no signs of dead or wounded, only "large sheets of frozen blood". The thieves had evidently come back to gather their slain.

Later that morning the news of the attack spread up and down the North Tyne valley. It took time to get a message to the owner, Colonel Ridley, in London but in the meantime men searched everywhere for the culprits. The body in the pedlar's pack was kept at the hall for inspection for a fortnight but no one could identify the body. Not a single clue was found as to who were the instigators of this organised burglary. Colonel Ridley, in due course, had the corpse of the pack buried at Bellingham.

The end piece to this bloody incident is a nice epitaph, for Hogg has written that the Colonel rewarded the defenders of his home liberally. Old Richard remained in the family during the rest of his life, and had a good salary for only saying prayers amongst the servants every night. Alice married a tobacconist in Hexham; whilst brave Edward was made the Colonel's head gamekeeper and was presented with a fine gold-mounted gun. I wonder if he ever loved this lovely firearm as much as he so obviously did his dear old Copenhagen?

Later Hogg says of Edward that:

"The Colonel afterwards procured him a commission in a regiment of foot where he suffered many misfortunes and disappointments. He was shot through the shoulder at the battle of Fontenoy, but recovered, and retiring on half-pay took a farm on the Scottish side of the Border. His character was that of a brave but rash officer, kind, generous and open hearted in all situations. I have often stood at his knee, Hogg writes, and listened with wonder and amazement to his stories of battles and sieges, but none of them ever pleased me better than that of The Long Pack".

L'ENVOI

During my recent pursuit of the occult in the two counties of Northumberland and Durham I have come across a remarkable number of, shall I say, little known ghosts, or apparitions, which have, in literature, been but lightly touched upon. Nancy Ridley, an authority on Northumbrian legend and folklore, has recorded in her most excellent book *Northumbrian Heritage* some fascinating hauntings. The ghost of Grizel Cochrane, a Scottish girl, is said to haunt the vicinity of Buckton, three miles north of Belford on the A.1 road. Grizel was the eighteen year old daughter of Sir John Cochrane of Ochiltree, son of the Earl of Dundonald. Cochrane was imprisoned in the Tolbooth Prison in Edinburgh, under sentence of death for his part in the rising of the Duke of Argyll. Knowing that her father's death warrant was on its way by coach from London to Edinburgh, Grizel crossed the Border, skilfully stole two pistols from the postman of Belford and then proceeded to waylay the coach and obtain her father's death warrant. This saved his life as urgent negotiations were then under way to have him reprieved but might not have been completed in time. The site of Grizel's haunting is now known as Grizie's Clump.

Another nearby supernatural being mentioned in *Northumbrian Heritage* is the Lady of Barmoor who on Lowick Moor is said to transfer herself into a white hare as midnight approaches. Hares, incidentally, are animals not infrequently linked with things occult. Amongst Miss Ridley's tales is one which concerns the haunting at Hardriding, a few miles west of Haydon Bridge on the north bank of the South Tyne. Hardriding, at, one time in the past, was a stronghold of the Ridley clan. The Hardriding ghost appears to have become active again in 1932 when one Bob English heard unearthly screams, thuds and bumps which were eventually to rouse the whole household. The ghost is supposed to be that of an ancient raider who was felled by an alert night watchman as he attempted to scale the walls. In the morning, after the intruder's repulse, only his hands and feet were found, wolves having devoured the remainder. On the anniversary of this deed, in the month of December, the Hardriding ghost is said to appear. Whether Bob English's recent experience was in any way connected with the episode when wolves still survived in Northumberland or whether some more modern poltergeistic phenomena roused Bob English is not stated. Nancy Ridley herself had the courage to stay a night at the seat of her ancestors during which occasion she appears to have had a quite tranquil sojourn.

Hundreds of cars per hour now hurtle along the east-west road from Newcastle to Carlisle and back. At one point near Ouston the road runs between the waterworks of Whittle Dene. Here the ghost of one Long Lonkin is still said to haunt Nafferton Tower. This gentleman appears to have been a pretty bad hat, a desperate character, in fact, for he was not only a thief, of whom there were many about in his day, but he was also the suspected murderer of a woman and child, a crime which rightly put him beyond the pale. Long Lonkin was accustomed to use the never completed Tower as one of his hideouts.

On May 1st 1971 *The Journal* of Newcastle upon Tyne published a paragraph on the ghost of Dorothy Forster. This stated that Dorothy, who lived in Jacobite times at the Lord Crewe Arms at Blanchland, Northumberland, rode down to London to rescue her brother Tom who was imprisoned in the Tower there. The Arms was once a monastery and then a private house occupied by the Forster family. Successful in her errand to release her brother, she brought him home to Blanchland where he was hidden in the priest's hole. This hide-out may still be seen today. Dorothy's spirit is said to haunt the premises searching for her brother who subsequently fled to France where so many other hunted Jacobites eventually went.

There is a book about Dorothy Forster, who, like Meg of Meldon, appears to have been a very considerable character. Dorothy's name is romantically linked with the Earl of Derwentwater whilst she lived at Blanchland. Dorothy appears to have had a longing to live at Bamburgh where another branch of her family resided, and who were Governors of the Castle. In this desire she appears to have been successful for legend says that her spiritual *alter ego* may also be seen at the Lord Crewe Arms at Bamburgh. Perhaps her spiritual self flits now from one extreme of the county to the other. Incidentally the autobiography of this unusual woman by Walter Besant is very scarce indeed. The public library in Morpeth has a copy but this may only be perused within this institution's precincts under the most strict surveillance for it is a most valuable document. Dorothy Forster is buried in the Forster vault at Bamburgh, so that those who tend to believe that one's spirit bides close to its earthly burial place would presumably lean towards Bamburgh as the site of this lady's ghost rather than the Lord Crewe Arms at Blanchland where the present apparition is frequently now stated to be that of a much earlier ghost, namely one of a monk.

Cross House stands in the middle of the village of Stamfordham in Northumberland. It is an attractive house built of lovely, rich-red, tudor bricks. Its sash windows are painted white and the front door is arched. Here live the Percys quite happily together with what appears to be a quaint poltergeist. Jervis Percy says his ghost is very unofficial. Its activities would appear to be mostly confined to the stable premises behind the house where the poltergeist makes play for the girl grooms. Like the Hedley Kow and that mischievous sprite The Cauld Lad of Hylton it seems to be a friendly, if slightly frivolous soul whose presence gives no sense of apprehension to the present inmates of Cross House. Whose ghost is this? Rumour says, as in the case of Dorothy Forster, that Derwentwater often visited Stamfordham in Jacobite times, and the sprite of Cross House is the spiritual relic of one of his grooms. Perhaps this is why the present lady equine-guardians get on so well with this unearthly being.

When I wrote of Meg of Meldon I made the statement that this was my nearest ghost. This is incorrect for I have now discovered one in the village only two houses away. The story is all very vague and the present owners of the Old Rectory in Whalton have never heard or seen it. I think that this ghost has in all probability been well and truly exorcised. Some say it was originally a monk whilst others claim it used to be a little old lady.

It was said to favour that part of the Rectory which was originally an old peile tower, and I know one lady here who once slept in the tower room and who says she felt uncomfortable. Certainly the late rector, Reverend Robert Watson, whom I knew well, had every intention of properly exorcising this manifestation. I cannot remember if he ever actually did so, but at any rate no recent appearances have been recorded.

A mile or so north of Meg's Meldon is Netherwitton Hall, the property of the well-known Trevelyan family. It is an attractive house set in glorious park-like surroundings. Netherwitton has always had its ghost, but of whose ghost it is no one seems to know. But then surely ghosts should be vague? The part I like best about Netherwitton's occult story is that of the window which would not stay shut. The late Eric Steel who lived at Netherwitton told me the story. Eric was quite unsuperstitious, a man who stood very firmly on his two big feet and who was the head of a vast industrial empire on Wearside. Eric when he took Netherwitton decided, with the landlord's consent, to eliminate the whole top floor as the house was over-roomed for modern usage. In the long row of the upper floor windows one refused to close. When shut at night it would be open again in the morning. Eric told one of the workmen, engaged on the renovations, to nail the window shut. In the morning the window was open. Eric now took the matter into his own hands; he secured some six-inch nails and nailed up the miscreant window. Next morning the nails had been wrenched out and the window once again was open! Rumour, who is so frequently a lying jade, has it that the ghost of Netherwitton, and presumably the one responsible for the open window, is that of a white lady. History tells that Cromwell stayed at Netherwitton in the summer of 1651 with his horseguards, nine regiments of foot and two of dragoons. During this visit something seems to have gone strangely awry for there is preserved in the County Archives in Newcastle upon Tyne a letter from Cromwell himself to Lady Thornton of Netherwitton ordering that she be paid as compensation the sum of £95 5s. 6d. This was a large sum in those days. Did some of Cromwell's licentious soldiery commit some dastardly crime? The likelihood is yes with so many men about and few so country wenches. Anyway the ghost of Netherwitton must have transferred her original chosen haunting site for in 1651 when Cromwell was there the Hall was a fourteenth century house and not the present Robert Trollope mansion.

    Here is the curious sequel to this story or, at least, I found it curious when I went recently to see the Hall. I had gone through the gate into the field facing the building so as to get a frontal view. I went towards the east end to find that the line of top-floor windows continued around the side of the house. Looking up at the three eastern windows I noticed that there were no light reflections in the far left-hand window. As I had my binoculars with me I was able to examine the windows carefully. The left hand one of the three had no glass. It was no more a window for it had been blocked up and apparently closely cemented and the sashes and the glazing bars had been painted in white on a jet-black background. This must have been the original window which was so hard to close; now it is quite incapable of being opened at all, and it is nearly impossible to distinguish the false from the other normal windows.

Printed in Great Britain
by Amazon